Junius McGehee

Glen Mary

A Catholic nove

Junius McGehee

Glen Mary
A Catholic nove
ISBN/EAN: 9783741189128
Manufactured in Europe, USA, Canada, Australia, Japa
Cover: Foto ©Lupo / pixelio.de

Manufactured and distributed by brebook publishing software (www.brebook.com)

Junius McGehee

Glen Mary

DEDICATION.

I dedicate to Our Lady of Perpetual Help this short story, not because it contains anything worthy of our loved and honored Lady, nor as a display of affection which silence would render more sacred, but as a short prayer that she who is so full of love and pity, and always ready to help poor erring nature, will take into her especial care her children who are willing to take upon themselves the grave responsibility of wives, from entering the holy state of matrimony without sufficient reflection, and what is still more vital, the sanction and approval of Holy Mother Church. Too many of our girls, alas! and parents also, think too little of the great change the few short words spoken by the priest make in the lives of the newly married, and that all their happiness here and eternal happiness hereafter, depends in a great measure upon the choice they make in their life companions. If the lesson contained in the ensuing volume will deter one young girl from marrying outside the Church, I will feel amply repaid for the labor it has cost me, and that our dear Lady has given a smile of approval to the work.

THE AUTHOR.

GLEN MARY.

CHAPTER I.

"COME, Mary, agree to my request. Let us both write out the future course of action we have resolved upon, when becoming wives tomorrow, and in ten years from now let us compare notes and see who is the wiser of the two. Here is pen, ink, and paper; I have already written mine; now listen while I read it to you:

'I, Estelle Norris, in becoming the wife of Alfred Fairfax, will, in no wise, give up my will; my peace of mind and my happiness must be his first and sole consideration. The words you *shall* and you *shan't*, you *must* and you *can't*, can never be used in addressing me.

'Witness hereto my seal and name,

'ESTELLE NORRIS.'

What do you think of those sentiments, Mary?"

"Why, Estelle, I think if those are really your sentiments, that it were far better for you if to-morrow were the day of your burial instead of your bridal."

"Well, pray enlighten me with your determination in becoming a wife. In other words what does that religion that you are continually harping upon say as regards the duty of wives."

"I like to hear you use the word *duty*, Estelle," said Mary, laughingly, "for it shows that you have some idea of right and wrong; but as regards what our church says, why, it teaches most emphatically that the wife is subject to the husband, that he is the head of the household, and that wives must love and obey their husbands."

"Then I suppose that you are marrying fully resolved upon becoming a slave, and that right or wrong, that your husband is to have his way in everything?"

"Where true love reigns there is no slavery in the question, but, as regards your other proposition, wouldn't it be better for him to have his way, even if wrong, than to live in continual broils, disputes, and contentions?"

"I'd contend till the breath left my body before I'd give up. I'll be no submissive wife, I assure you, but as it is getting late and we have to change both our name and place of residence early in the morning, we had better say good night."

"Oh! not before you promise me that you'll not marry with those wicked resolutions filling your heart, dear Estelle," said the girl addressed, going up to her and pleadingly throwing her arms around her neck.

"Mary, may I tell you something confidentially?" asked Estelle in a softened voice.

"Oh yes, anything," answered Mary encouragingly; "say anything you please, dear Estelle."

"Well it is only this—that you *are a big* goose," and with a laugh at the pained expression in the gentle eyes looking up into hers, she lightly ran out of the room.

From the fragmentary conversation given above, the reader can understand that the two girls speaking are on the morrow to assume the grave responsibility of wives. As our story differs from novels generally, in beginning with the marriage, where others usually end, it also differs in the particular of but one heroine, for ours has two; and as these intended brides are our heroines, we must go back a year or two to introduce them properly, to make our reader as interested in their future welfare as we are ourselves.

If it is a feminine reader she will want to know the first thing their age and their style. If masculine, their place of residence and the amount for which they have credit at the bank. Giving the female the preference, we will satisfy her curiosity first, and as quickly as possible the male's.

They have both just reached their twentieth year. One has eyes the color of that indescribable purple that adorns the brows of distant mountains at evening's close, with a pleading look for love and protection in them that goes straight to the heart; her complexion is almost snowy in its whiteness, that flushes, not blushes, love to mantle; long braids of yellowish hair, strongly tinged with auburn, coil in graceful profusion around her shapely head; while in the face there is an expression of so much gentleness, purity, and innocence, that had Raphael seen her, he would have tried to have secured her for a model. In stature she was rather below the medium height. Her cousin—the other lady—was her exact opposite in everything save beauty; in that she rivalled her, nay, to the most of eyes, excelled her. Where one was a lovely blonde, the other was a brilliant brunette. Being cousins german, both their names was Norris—the blonde, Mary; the brunette, Estelle.

Both are orphans—Estelle rich in worldly goods, Mary almost destitute. The year before our story opens, Mary graduated with all the honor that the Convent of C—— confers on its graduates. She could hardly carry the many premiums that were awarded her in her different studies. When the graduate's medal was handed, she was pleased, but when she was called to receive the crown of honor given for deportment, one of those flushes we have spoken of suffused her cheek. Her emotion was very great, for she had not even dreamed that she would receive the crown, and who can tell how grateful she felt to those kind nuns, who for eighteen years had shielded and protected her from every harm—for Mary was homeless. The day after the Distribution she felt the misery contained in that little word in its full force, when the questions for the first time suggested themselves, what must I do for a living? what will my future be? True, she could stay on with the kind Sisters, who never by word, look, or sign, ever made her feel the necessity of leaving them. On the contrary, they had spoken about her assisting in some of their classes, as if, as a matter of course, she was going to stay on with them. But well Mary knew that this was but a subterfuge of charity, that these ladies who were so capable themselves did not need her to assist them. No! duty bade her go away, and no longer burthen with her support the noblest women on earth, who are so properly named "Sisters of Charity." Oh! if it had been but God's will for her to have been one she would have been saved all this pain, but the great privilege of being among the chosen few who "shall follow the Lamb whithersoever He goeth" was denied to her, and she must go out into the big, cold world, unknown and companionless, to fight life's battles. Are bread, meat, and clothes—the three essentials—then so very hard to get, that they cost all this suffering? she asked herself. A sad smile was the only answer she could summon. Whilst she is still deep in the depths of her first sorrow, a note is handed her, which after reading she felt that a kind Providence had sent. It read as follows:

"*My dear Niece:*

"No doubt you will be surprised to hear that you have an aunt living, who is now pleading with you to come to her at once. The Superioress of your Convent will explain everything to you, as I am too feeble to write more. Your affectionate aunt,

"A. S. NORRIS.

"Miss Mary Norris."

With both delight and surprise, Mary listened while it was explained to her that her mother's sister-in-law—the lady from whom the note was received—was yet alive, but had always remained unknown to her on account of Mary's religion, as Mrs. Norris, up to a very late date, abhorred anything and everything that pertained to Catholicism, but that now she was a convert herself, and ardently wished for her niece-in-law to visit her.

In a few days Mary bade adieu to her childhood's home, to the kind Sisters who, with anxious care, had shielded her from every harm, and to the gray-haired pastor who had indeed been a father to her, to commence life's journey, alone and friendless.

CHAPTER II.

THE magnificence of the mountain scenery—seen for the first time by Mary—and the beauty of the spacious grounds that surrounded her aunt's stately home were so captivating, that she was not prepared for the shock that awaited her when ushered into the invalid's presence.

She found her reclining on a divan near one of the open windows, viewing a lovely landscape that stretched far out in the distance until lost in a stream of mad water that rushed murmuringly through the valley, enhancing the picturesqueness of the place, that even without it seemed to whisper of that other country, the beauties of which hath not entered the heart of man.

"Ah! so you have come at last?" spoke Mrs. Norris, as she languidly raised herself to welcome her niece.

"Yes, and am so glad to know that I have a dear aunt living who really wishes to see me," answered Mary, going up to the invalid and tenderly embracing her. I believed myself entirely alone in the world until your dear note came, and I am ——" here Mary suddenly stopped as she for the first time took in with a rapid glance the emaciated form before her, and heard the hollow cough that spoke so plainly of the grave, and sighed to think that she had found her but to lose her. Mrs. Norris noted the compassionate expression that came into the glad eyes looking down upon her, and answered it, saying:

"Don't pity me, child, for every hour of life that's left to me should be filled with thanksgiving for the great mercy that has been vouchsafed me, after the life of worldliness, and regardlessness of my Creator, that I have led. You have, of course, heard that of my conversion, and that by God's grace I am now a member of the One, Holy, Catholic, Apostolic Church, for which I feel I can never be grateful enough; but let me explain why I have neglected you so long, and now when I have but a short time to live, sent for you. Your mother and myself grew up together, and from our earliest girlhood were fast friends. When fully grown we married brothers on the same day; our friendship continued for several years afterwards, until our little girls were born—you and your cousin Estelle."

"Oh! have I a cousin, too?" interrupted Mary in glad surprise.

"Yes," sadly answered Mrs. Norris, "but let me continue. In selecting names for our babes, I was astonished when your mother declared her intention of calling you after the mother of God; but when she said that she was going to have you baptized a Catholic I was both shocked and distressed—so much so that to quiet me it was necessary to call in a physician. My abhorrence of the act did not prevent it, however, and you were not only baptized, but your mother also. On the day that she was received into the Church I made a vow that I would never speak to her again; a vow that some demon made me keep, and who hardened my heart to the many overtures made by your mother to reach it.

"Our estrangement and my obstinacy at length told on your parent's health, and your father removed his wife to a kindlier atmosphere. The change was a most unfortunate one, for, in less than a year afterwards, that fearful scourge, yellow fever, deprived you of both father and mother, and you were given in charge to the good sisters who have reared you so tenderly, whilst only an infant. Her last words was a kind message to me, promising that she would pray for me in Heaven. Shortly before, she had sent me a little volume which she implored me to read, but which, with my usual obstinacy, I put away, and it remained unopened until my physician told me that I, too, must die. Oh, how awful! to die before I had begun to live, for, had I not been dead to grace and the true faith all my life, merciful Lord! What did death mean to me but eternal death, eternal suffering, eternal loss. Oh, my dear child! it seems to me that the eternity of the life to come will not be long enough to do away with the horror that I endured when I was first told that death was inevitable, and that in a few days I must receive the dread summons. Some pitying angel made me think of the little book your mother had sent me, taking it in my hands, I pressed it to my lips, and felt that it was sent as an especial mercy to me. I opened it and my eyes fell on the words: 'Know ye the truth, and the truth will set you free.' Eagerly I read on, page after page, it seemed that my long lost friend was speaking to me again. She was surely praying for me, for, when I laid down the small volume, I was a Catholic in belief, shortly afterwards I became one in act, and all horror of death, thank God, vanished. My only anxiety now is for the living, for my poor child. On her account I sent for you. I have been informed that you are a devout Catholic, and well instructed; for the nineteen years of your cousin's life, she has been reared in entire ignorance of her Creator. I taught her that it was not well for bright eyes and rosy lips to see or speak of death, that it had naught to do with her glad young being, my chief aim, since her birth, was to shield her from pain or knowledge of misery. The consequence of my great mistake is, that now she will not listen to the heavenly truths that I try to instil into her mind. She laughs at what I say, and evidently thinks that her mother is fast approaching her dotage. She is engaged to a young man whom I once thought was, in every way, worthy of her affection, but oh! Mary, as your end approaches, how vain all things earthly seem, compared with those which are eternal. The attractions that I once thought so great, are now to me his greatest objections. He is young, and, although alone in the world, his ancestors have distinguished themselves both in war and in peace, he is the possessor of unlimited wealth, is a refined and cultivated gentleman, addicted to no vice, but alas! is as ignorant as Estelle of the Author of his being. No wonder you weep tears of compassion for me, dear Mary, for I am truly punished. Ah, there the poor child comes now," and she pointed towards a couple, a lady and gentleman, approaching on horseback.

As Mary closely scanned the girl pointed out to her, she was compelled to acknowledge that she never saw a fairer specimen of the softer sex. Arrayed in a dark green riding habit, fitting to a nicety her light graceful figure, with hat and plume to match, she sprang lightly from her horse and, after kissing her hand to her lover, ran laughingly into the room, exclaiming: "I have stayed an unconscionable length of time, hav'nt I, mamma?" She stopped in astonishment to look at Mary.

"This is your cousin, that I have told you I was expecting, Estelle," spoke Mrs. Norris.

"Well, we begin our acquaintance with me your debtor," said Estelle, going up to Mary and embracing her, "for I see from mamma's animated face that she has not missed me during my long absence, thanks to you."

After a few commonplace remarks, they were summoned to the dining-room — a room complete in all its appointments. Never before did Mary see such an array of silver; the magnificence of the whole service dazed her, and she sighed to think that death was coming amid everything so grandly beautiful. After returning to the sick room, Mrs. Norris asked Mary to read to her; the book selected was a volume of "Butler's Lives of the Saints." After reading one or two of the most entertaining and instructive of the lives, a deep groan from her aunt made her look up, and to her surprise she saw that Estelle was sleeping soundly.

CHAPTER III.

"WILL morning never come?" asked the poor weary invalid, a few months after Mary's arrival.

"Yes, auntie, it is almost here now," answered Mary as she slightly opened a shutter to let in the first rays the aurora was casting forth.

"O blessed rays! blest harbinger of day! do I again behold thee? During the long and terrible hours of the night I despaired of ever seeing thee again!"

"Please don't talk so despondingly, dear aunt," interrupted the girl, "you seem much quieter just now than you have for a long time, and you have not coughed for several hours."

"I will never cough again, dear child, and physically I will never suffer more. I want you to attend mass this morning, and ask Father Kain to come over and administer the last sacraments, for I feel that it would be wrong to put off the reception of them longer; but before you go promise me once more, that you will do all you can to atone for my heartless neglect of Estelle."

"Oh, dear aunt, I promise you to do all that I can to bring your child to the knowledge of the true faith, and believe me the task will not be hard with you and my mother praying for us in heaven," said Mary, with quivering lips and eyes full of tears, for in the little while she had known her, she had become fondly attached to this patient sufferer, who was once her mother's dearest friend.

If we will enter the room a few hours afterwards we will see the Priest in the sweet character of consoler, and administering the last sacraments of the Church to the dying; and why do we find him at this solemn hour so different from all the others who call themselves ministers of the Most High? Ah, that's a question easily answered—simply because he is the only one of them all who obeys the command, so plainly given, in that holy book which all receive as the inspired word of God: "Is any man sick among you? let him bring in the priests of the Church, and let them pray over him, anointing him with oil in the name of the Lord; and the prayer of faith shall save the sick man, and the Lord shall raise him up, and if he be in sins they shall be forgiven him."— *St. James*, v. 14, 15.

Mrs. Norris felt forcibly the great mercy that was vouchsafed her, and whilst yet full of the delight of possessing her Saviour, and with a heart on fire with love, she sweetly and peacefully sank to rest, let us hope, not for even a moment to be separated from the merciful Redeemer, who in obedience to man's call had come to console her in her agony.

Mary was sorely grieved when she felt that she had lost forever this dear friend, but it was different with Estelle. She did not seem to realize her great loss, and said she could not think of her mother as dead, only absent on a visit. Mary stayed her own grief to comfort the daughter, whose bereavement was irreparable, and told her that her thinking so was the first mercy that her mother had obtained for her from the Author of Mercy, and that that was the way we should all think of our departed dear ones, as only away for a time, and who sooner or later we would join.

Time, that waits for no man, and whose wings never lag or tire, flew on in spite of the great change that death had wrought in a once happy family, and one year after the gentle mother and kind aunt was laid to rest, if we repair thither, we will find the daughter and niece in the flower garden, conversing with Estelle's betrothed and another gentleman.

Although as we enter we are struck by the beauty of the flowers, which are rich and rare, choice exotics of every clime, blooming in wasteful profusion, and scenting the air with delicious perfume far into the distance, still we have to pause in admiration of the two couples who are culling the sweets.

Robed in heavy black, Estelle stood leaning against a trellis, twining into a wreath a running vine covered with bright bloom, that she was holding. It was full of beauty, but to the enamored eye of the tall man beside her, not near so lovely as the fair girl wreathing it. He must have told her so, for a bright blush suffuses her face, and in evident embarrassment she carelessly throws and encircles Mary's head with it, and laughingly says:

"It contrasts with Mary's light locks beautifully. Oh, how vastly becoming!"

To Mary who had not mingled long enough in society to lose the natural timidity of her character, and which is so attractive in young girls, to be thus brought under the steady gaze of all the eyes fixed upon her, it was really painful. She hastily raised her hands to remove the vine, which she soon found was quite a difficult task, for its tendrils seemed to be playing hide and seek in her wavy tresses. Of herself she could not accomplish it, and was obliged to receive the assistance of the gentleman at her side, who carefully uncoiled its tenacious hold. When loosened, Mary, who was greatly annoyed at the whole proceeding, rather roughly, it must be confessed, threw it to the ground. Alas for human calculation—one of its sprays which had not before been noticed, had encircled itself around a chain, hidden under Mary's collar, and it, together with a locket attached, fell with the wreath to the ground.

"Oh, don't! please don't!" exclaimed Mary in terror, as she saw the locket by its fall was opened. "I'll pick it up; oh, please let me!"

But Dr. Graham, the gentleman addressed, forgetful of Lord Chesterfield's idea of politeness as regards requests, stooped forward, picked it up, and returned it to its owner, but not before he had caught a glimpse of his own face in the trinket, and he remembered that about two years before he had given this locket, containing a small likeness of himself, to Mrs. Norris. From the pleased expression of his face, the unexpected finding of it was not disagreeable, and he quickly followed the now weeping girl into the veranda and, doctor fashion, waited until the painful emotion, which was mastering her, had been conquered, and then told how he had intended leaving home and country the following day because, like Byron, he could love but one, and that she was so cold and formal, repelling all his advances so decidedly, that but for the happy accident of the locket falling, he could never have spoken to her of his great love. Vainly she tried to explain that it was Estelle who had clasped the chain, holding the locket around her neck, only that morning where it had remained forgotten. He would listen to nothing but an answer to his wooing, and when, at length, she spoke, she still wept, but they were happy tears that coursed down her flushed cheeks.

CHAPTER IV.

IT is time for us to say a word or two concerning the two gentlemen who are destined to figure quite conspicuously in this life history.

Alfred Fairfax, the betrothed of Estelle, is a gentleman in every sense of the word, a stately and elegant gentleman, whose kind heart is full of love and tenderness for the young girl who is to give herself into his keeping. He was a man of great intellect, of vast resources, and unbounded ambition, was sole possessor of the finest estate in the neighborhood, and the master of Dunreath Abbey, which with its spacious grounds, numerous statues, laughing fountains, and Doric architecture made it grandly beautiful, and the delight and pride of the surrounding country.

To make Estelle Norris the mistress of his handsome home was the one thought of his life. His had been a lonely life; all his near relatives, save his father, died whilst he was still a child, and in the last few years his aged father had been added to his list of departed friends, which left him lonely indeed, and he longed for the time to come, with a weary longing, when he could clasp the rare jewel he thought Estelle to his heart, and see love and harmony preside in his princely home once more.

Alas! poor youth. How was it with Estelle? She, too, longed for the short time to elapse when she could reign mistress of the grand old abbey, and be the envied of all the envious. One thought of what a home would be without religion never entered into the mind of either, and before our story closes we will see how it fared with these two young people, who placed their happiness solely upon the fleeting things of earth.

The man Mary was to marry was similar to Alfred in many respects; he was young, handsome, and rich, and would inherit an estate equal, if not superior, to Dunreath Abbey. He was unfortunate enough to be an only child, and was not an exception to the rule that "an only child is a spoilt one." Every wish of his heart, every desire of his life, had been gratified by indulgent parents, who seemed to live but to anticipate his many wants.

His father, Col. Gilmore Graham, was the Washington of his country—fairly idolized by its people, and also regarded as a second Solomon. All disputes were brought to him to settle; his advice was sought upon all occasions, little or big; and woe to the man who would go contrary to the advice of their magnate. Great was the amazement of his admirers, when it was understood that he had consented to his son's marrying, and marrying a papist, so some of the most audacious went to him for an explanation. He told them that when first his son broached the subject of his marriage that he would not listen to it, for he had, as he thought, two insurmountable objections; one, that Mary was poor, he did not like unequal matches, it savored too much of mercenary motives, the other was her being a

Catholic. Here was an old man who, perhaps for the sixty years of his life, never once bent his knee in fealty to his Creator, and who knew no more of religion than perhaps that there is a God, objecting to Mary's being a Catholic, and his fawners looked on admiringly and were more convinced than ever of the wisdom of Col. Graham. "But," he continued, "I am but flesh and blood, and whilst I deplored his choice, for the sake of his peace I consented, for I could not endure to see the suffering that I was causing my only child."

Mrs. Graham—his wife—was his exact opposite; was one of those trembling, uncertain little women, that seem to be but the reflex of the lives around them, with no opinion of their own, who pass through the world disliked by none, but with few friends and no admirers; who are invariably spoken of as *poor* Mrs. So-and-so, upon whom a lavish amount of sympathy is expended, though if the persons expending it were asked why they bestowed it, they could not answer the question. Certainly poor Mrs. Graham, as she was always styled, needed none, for she was a proud and devoted mother; a loving and beloved wife; in the enjoyment of perfect health, with no wish ungratified; and why she should have received the compassion denied to worthier objects we are at a loss to determine.

The only other member of the family was a widowed sister-in-law of the colonel's, and never did royal queen, absolute in power, reign with more undisputed sway than did Sister Sallie over Glen Mary, the home of the Grahams.

The morning of the 20th of October, 18—, has come at last, and two brides are breathing the vows that bind them indissolubly to man. Very fair the cousins look as they stand repeating the few short words that no after reflection, no desire, howsoever great—*no*, not even breaking hearts, can ever unsay. Oh! brides, do you ever consider the awfulness of what you do when you bind yourselves, before God, to love, honor and obey a man you scarcely know, and of whose inner life you have not dreamt? Earthly love! how many sacrifices are daily offered at thy shrine amid the acclamations of surrounding friends, and gratified mammas and papas, who smile to see their friend and daughter taking upon herself the fearful obligation to love and serve poor, frail, weak, sinful man, with his thousand vexing peculiarities, his propensity to vice, and his dreadful stubbornness in declaring himself sole arbitrator of the young life committed to his charge.

After the few moments were over that changed the whole current of their lives, they are driven to the nearest station, from whence they will travel for a few weeks before settling down in the usual humdrum manner of most married people. How often in after years did they look back to those few days with an impatient longing for their return; thus proving "that a sorrow's crown of sorrow is in remembering happier things."

CHAPTER V.

GLEN Mary is dressed in her gayest apparel to welcome the son and heir, and his young wife. The carriage containing the bridal party has already been descried in the distance, which fact makes the immediate family repair to the balcony to, as it were, hasten the arrival. Let us scan their features as they stand there impatiently watching the approaching vehicle, for, in the expectancy of the meeting, they are off their guards, and perhaps, taking them unawares, we may learn something of the people with whom it is Mary's lot to associate in the future.

Col. Graham is bending forward, slightly leaning over the railing, with eyes strained in the direction of the carriage. Judging from his position he is all eagerness to welcome the young girl who will claim him as father, to his heart, but the set expression around his mouth, the annoyance expressed in the look of fixed determination in his face, makes us fear for the young bride. The wife and mother stands at his side, in painful perplexity, for, as her husband's face is hidden from her, she can't for the life of her decide whether he is secretly annoyed or silently rejoicing, and consequently don't know whether she should be glad or sad. She gives a sigh of relief as she determines to await events, and be guided by them. There is but one more face to scan, and as we look into the features of rare beauty possessed by the sister-in-law, and note the expression of the handsome black eyes watching the approach of the party, we shudder at what we read there, and in our hearts offer up a fervent prayer for the young wife's future peace and happiness.

The carriage has reached the balcony, and descending from it are Alfred Fairfax and the two cousins. George is already clasped in the arms of his parents and Aunt Sallie. After a warm embrace from each, he turns to introduce his timid bride, who is tremblingly advancing, and who, for the first time, he thought awkward; a quick glance of compassion from the sister-in-law makes him aware that the first impression produced by his wife is not a favorable one. Mary is also conscious of it, and of becoming rapidly mesmerized by a pair of brilliant black eyes that note her every movement, and sank into a deep lethargy which she found it impossible to arouse herself from, and it was a relief to all when the day was over, and the carriages announced that were to take them to Dunreath Abbey, where a large party of the fashionable and great were assembled to welcome its mistress. Shortly after their departure, Mrs. Col. Graham turned to her sister-in-law and hesitatingly asked, "What do you think of my son's wife, Sister Sallie?" Away down in her heart there was a voice pleading for the poor young creature, that had come to her for love and protection, and she awaited the answer to her question in some trepidation for fear the kind voice would be hushed.

"What do I think of Mary? Well, as she came up the steps this morning, I was reminded of a poor frightened doe that finds herself surrounded by dogs, ready to tear her to pieces, and so she appeared to me all evening, until——"

"Oh! I'm rejoiced that you do not think her deep and designing," interrupted Mrs. Graham. "I will try to make the little girl feel more at home when she comes back. But I broke in upon you; what were you going to say—until, until what, Sister Sallie?"

"Until dinner was served, and then I saw a look in those modestly downcast eyes that I did not like. It was when she surveyed the many pieces of our family silver, and I noted that each piece was inspected separately and intently; the look seemed to say, 'all these belong to me,' and a smile of mercenary pride lit up her face. The thought struck me, sister, that a young bride that could think of such things the same hour that she was first introduced to her husband's home, thought more of his wealth and her future prospects than she did of him or his family; and I also noticed that she ignored you and brother equally as she did me—not addressing a word to any of us during the entire day. Evidently she thinks us in the way, and that we have no business at Glen Mary."

"Oh, then she is a deep, designing woman, which is all hidden under the appearance of a timid, modest girl, and it was this false modesty that took in my poor son. Ah! the vile wretch; I'll warn the Colonel, and tell him that you told me."

"No, you must tell him nothing of the kind, for I have told you nothing but that she seemed embarrassed and frightened. As for the mere thought or passing reflection I had about her, you must not repeat it."

"I will not, Sister Sallie, if you object, but is it not awful to have to bring this villain into our happy family?"

Sister Sallie murmured something like yes, but Mrs. Graham could not catch the answer; and from thenceforth the only person at Glen Mary at all inclined to favor Mary, closed and barred her heart firmly against her. Alas! poor young wife.

The party at Dunreath Abbey, which was quite a brilliant affair, was over, and carriage after carriage was bearing away the tired revellers. In one there were only two persons, and if a third were added, he could not believe that the loud, excited tones of voice issuing from the gentleman occupant, and which were addressed to the lady by his side, could possibly be those of Dr. George Graham, and the lady his bride of only three weeks; but true it was, and he was rudely upbraiding her for the disagreeable impression he saw she had created at the Glen.

"But, Dr. Graham," she faltered, "indeed I could not help it; I felt so very, very miserable."

"And pray, madam, what was to cause you to feel miserable on the evening you were first introduced as the future mistress of Glen Mary? I assure you, that that is an honor that the first lady in the State would be proud of, and there was no one present wanting in respect."

"Oh! Dr. Graham, I never thought of that, and perhaps I was not grateful enough for the beautiful home you have given me—but George—" here a sob stopped her utterance—"I never had a father or mother, and you don't know how I dreaded meeting yours, for fear that they would not receive me as a daughter and allow me to love them."

"Yes, you took good care, madam, that they would not receive you as a child, and it's little love that they can expect from the cold, inanimate creature you appeared all evening!" Here her sobs interrupted him, and as the carriage had stopped in front of the door he said no more, but assisted his bride into the house which had already become a terror to her.

CHAPTER VI.

THE next morning was bright, balmy and clear; birds were warbling in every bush, even the fountains within the inclosure seemed to be playing sweet music, as Mary returned from Mass, which had been celebrated in the village near. She paused at one of the fountains to watch its bright, glad waters, and was busy symbolizing them with time, whose moments passed as rapidly away as the drops of water fell into the basin, and which like the drops would never return again, when a hand was laid upon her shoulder, and she turned to confront Col. Graham.

"Good morning, my daughter. Why, you seem to be an early riser, I saw you returning from a walk just now; where have you been?"

"I was at church in the village, sir, where I went to assist at early Mass."

"Went to do what I believe you call worshipping God. Well, I must say that you Catholics are very zealous, when you can arouse yourselves as early as this to worship. Why do you attend church so early?"

"Because, sir, the first part of every day should be given to God."

"How, child, do you know that there is such a spirit as this God that you give yourself so much trouble to serve?"

"Know there is a God!" asked Mary in surprise.

"Aha! daughter, you never thought of that, daughter, did you? and here you go on from day to day giving yourself infinite trouble to worship your God, and when you are asked how you know there is a God, you have nothing to say."

"I had nothing to say, sir, because I was astonished at your question. Know there is a God! Why, can you look upon the grand expanse of the heavens, see the sun in all his majesty lighting up the world whilst the day lasts, and at night the milder and gentler moon take its place, and see this light returning day after day and night after night, and not know that some hand greater than man's has placed them there? And how can you account for the wonderful machinery of man; the smallest part of the body, the heart, being the seat of life, and that from it ebbs and flows all the blood that fills our veins; and for our walking and talking, thinking and dreaming, sleeping and waking, without acknowledging that a greater power than ours has made us, and made us even a mystery to ourselves. And then, sir, do you not feel the goodness of God every day and every hour?"

"All that is very true, my child, but before I can believe there is a God, I must have some visible demonstration of the fact: it is not enough for me to feel there is one, like it seems to be for you. You know the old adage, 'seeing is believing.'"

"What is that, sir, which is raising the hair from your brow, and why, since we have been talking, have you attempted several times to save your hat from falling off?"

"Why, it is rather a strong breeze; but I don't see the point you are driving at."

"You told me just now, sir, that seeing only was believing with you."

"Well, I did say as much, but what has that got to do with the breeze?"

"I didn't know that you could see the breeze, sir, I thought you only felt it."

Here the Colonel broke out into a hearty laugh, and acknowledged that he was beaten, and then remained silent, thinking that this young girl had brought more forcibly to his mind the knowledge of God than all the deep philosophical works he had ever examined on the subject, and he wondered at it until the bell summoned to breakfast.

Very beautiful did Mary look as she entered the dining room, to the amazement of all, leaning upon her father-in-law's arm.

A deep flush dyed her usually pale cheek, called there by her enthusiasm, but as she advanced with a pleasant smile to her mother-in-law, to give the morning greetings, she was met with such an icy repulse that the blood forsook her face, and she silently took her seat at the table, again feeling conscious that those brilliant black eyes were fastened intently upon her.

She tried several times to shake off the feeling that was rapidly mastering her, but in vain. She was plunged into the depths of despair by a cold, rebuking glance from her husband. After drinking a cup of tea and eating half a roll, she excused herself and left the room, followed by Dr. Graham.

When they were gone the Colonel turned to Sister Sallie, as if for her opinion of Mary. That lady was very nice in her choice of words as she was giving her opinion, but ended by saying, "that it was to be hoped that she married George only for love and had not thought of his money."

"By the gods!" exclaimed the Colonel, "if I thought it was for his money she married him, he should never have a cent of it as long as he called her wife."

"Well, husband, if you had noticed how her eyes glistened as she surveyed our silver service yesterday, which was remarked by one she didn't know was watching her, you would have very little doubt of the truth of what Sister Sallie has said."

"Said! why, I have said nothing, and I am sure that I would be the last person in the world to injure, in your estimation, your son's wife."

"We know that you intended to do nothing of the kind, Sister Sallie," returned the Colonel, "but this is not the first time we have been indebted to your wise sagacity for information, but we will drop the subject now."

"Wife, I forgot to tell you that Caroline will be here to-morrow, and will probably stay some months with us. She will be accompanied by a young lady friend, so the letter I got this morning stated."

"Oh! I am glad to hear that Sister Caroline will be here so soon," said both the Mrs. Grahams in one voice, for which the Colonel gave each a grateful look, and arose from the table.

We must say a word or two about the expected

guests at Glen Mary before finishing the chapter. Mrs. Caroline Graham, widow of the Colonel's half-brother, Robert Graham, was a woman about thirty-five years of age, but she looked at least ten years younger. She was extremely beautiful; a stately woman, whose slightest motion was the studied perfection of ease and grace; in disposition she was cold and unapproachable, and she seemed to live upon the pride she took in all that related to the honor of the house of Graham. Her haughtiness and reserve made her few friends, though she passed through the world admired by all, for she was never known to be guilty of the least unladylike act; she was a lady, always and everywhere, although she had a habit of wondering with her cold grey eyes, how you could so forget yourself as to speak from impulse, which was disagreeable, and it was surprising to see how carefully her eyes were watched by the persons she was with, to note whether or not the words they spoke were disapproved of or otherwise.

The friend that accompanied her was a joyous, bright young girl, who had just escaped from what she called "the thraldom of school life," and whose invalid mother had placed her under the care and supervision of Mrs. Graham (whom she vastly admired) in the vain hope that she could mould the exuberant spirits of her daughter Viola, into the perfect calm of her own. Mrs. Graham was also to bring to the Glen her only child, an attractive, winning girl of some fourteen years, who insensibly won the affections of every one, whose name was Coralie.

CHAPTER VII.

SEVERAL months have elapsed since Mary's arrival at her husband's home, and, as we look in upon her this dark, dreary, rainy evening, we see at a glance that she is still unhappy, because she is still misunderstood. She forms a lovely picture, leaning against the railing which surrounds the gallery, with her head gracefully thrown back, as she pensively surveys the war of the elements in the heavens above, a running rose vine near lends her an additional charm, by resting several of its flowers amidst her brown ringlets which, by the contrast, makes them appear even more beautiful than usual, so Col. Graham thinks, as he, struck by her beauty, calls Mrs. Caroline's attention to her. They stand for a few moments silently watching and admiring her, when one word spoken by a low voice near them dissolves the spell of beauty; that word was "actress," and Sister Sallie the person that uttered it.

"Why do you say that, Sister Sallie?" asked the Colonel, slightly annoyed at the disagreeable interruption.

"Say what, brother?"

"Say that Mary is an actress!"

"I say that she was an actress! indeed I said no such thing; she only reminded me of one I saw acting innocence."

The Colonel, still displeased, turned and walked away, leaving the two ladies together.

For a few moments they remained silent, when Sister Sallie again spoke.

"Caroline, I have a very disagreeable duty to perform, and it is to warn you of the influence that that papist," pointing to Mary, "is exerting over Coralie and Viola. You must, my dear sister, keep those children away from the tempter, or, presently, you will have them imbued with all the superstitions and errors of the Romish Church."

"Why, you cannot mean to say that she would try to instil any of the errors of her doctrine into the mind of my angel child?"

"All that I know, Caroline, is that this morning I heard her tell Coralie she must not speak of the Virgin Mary as of any ordinary woman, that she must remember that she was the Mother of God, and we were told to call her blessed."

"Oh! Sister Sallie, I am so truly thankful to you for telling me. I will go at once and prohibit all future intercourse between her and my child, or after awhile I would see my darling adoring pictures, statues, crucifixes, &c." Saying this, the lady turned and walked towards Mary with more haste in her step than was her wont, but, with her usual good breeding, she addressed her niece-in-law in the low, modulated tone of voice peculiarly her own:

"I am very sorry to hear, Mary, that you have been inculcating some of the teachings of your church—which, excuse me for saying, I believe erroneous—into the mind of my child, and I have come to request that you will desist from trying to proselyte her."

"Why, Aunt! I am ignorant of having ever attempted it, so please tell me how I have incurred your displeasure in this particular!"

"Were you not, this very morning, attempting to make her imagine the Virgin Mary equal to God, and even superior? this is your offence."

Mary opened her large brown eyes in wonder as she answered: "I tried to make her think our Blessed Mother equal to God? Why, there is no Catholic, be he ever so ignorant, who would dare insult his Creator by raising his creature to a level with Him! Your words shock me. The bare idea is abhorrent to every Catholic feeling and sentiment."

"I hope, Mary, that you do not deny that you call her the Mother of God, and that your Church teaches you to salute her as blessed?"

"I certainly do call her the Mother of God, for is she not the mother of the *Word*, who in the beginning was with God, and was God, and who became man to save us, and if I call her blessed I do no more than the angel, the messenger of the Most High, did when he saluted her in these words: 'Hail! full of grace, the Lord is with thee. Blessed art thou amongst women.' If one of God's angels can call her blessed without offence to God, surely one of his creatures on earth can do the same. And then has not our Blessed Mother said, when speaking to her cousin Elizabeth of the great things that 'He that was mighty' had done for her, that 'from henceforth all generations shall call me blessed?'"

"True. I'll acknowledge, Mary, that I have not given the subject sufficient reflection; but tell me now—you cannot believe that Jesus Christ, whom we believe and know to be God, would be subject to a woman?"

"Dear aunt, do we, anywhere in the Scripture, read of Jesus transgressing the law of God, and does not one of these laws command us to honor our father and mother? Surely the Divine Maker of laws would not set us an example of breaking them; and we do read that He returned with His parents into Nazareth and was subject to them."

"Well, I will not discuss the subject further; but, Mary, I again ask you to promise me that you will not explain any of the tenets of your faith to my child."

"Certainly I will promise you, Aunt Caroline, unless Coralie should come to me and insist on an explanation; in that case I would not like to refuse the information she asks for."

"Oh! what shall I do!" exclaimed the lady, now really excited. "How can I save my darling. I will have to leave Glen Mary at once." And she rushed almost frantically to her room to make preparations for her immediate departure

That was a sad evening in the history of Mary's life, when it was ascertained that Mrs. Graham was leaving the Glen owing to an insult she had received from her

The Colonel swore until he was blue in the face, and told George that if he did not make his wife apologize and retract what she had said offensive to

his sister and to his guest, that he would see which
should leave; if either had to go, Mary should be
the one. Mrs. Colonel Graham was in deep distress,
judging from the sighs and groans that escaped her,
whilst Sister Sallie's black eyes were prettily hid
behind a lace handkerchief which she held gracefully
before them.

Mary saw that she was the innocent cause of all
this unhappiness and disturbance in a family noted
for its oneness and affection, but she felt powerless to
remove it. Whilst she was so reflecting upon it, and
praying for strength from on high, Dr. Graham
entered her chamber, with every feeling of resent-
ment within him excited to the highest pitch; he
stood, regarding his wife for a few minutes, in
speechless anger, and then, in that low, subdued
tone, which makes you tremble at the amount of
emotion it is intended to conceal, asked:

"Is what I hear true, madam, that you have
insulted my aunt in my father's house, and she his
invited guest?"

"I have been unfortunate enough, George, to give
your aunt offence; but, my dear husband, I did not
intend it," said Mary in a low, tearful voice.

"Stop, madam," he replied; "nothing can excuse
your unpardonable conduct. Aunt Sallie, who was
an eye-witness of your rudeness, has told us that,
when Aunt Caroline had found out that you had
been tampering with her child, she went to you in
her usual mild manner and gently requested you to
desist, which you most positively and emphatically
refused to do."

"Oh! George," sobbed the poor wife, "Aunt Sallie is mistaken. I did not intend proselyting Coralie, and I told Aunt Caroline so. I only said that if she insisted on my answering any questions concerning my religion, I would be obliged to answer them."

"I suppose your religion teaches you to be a stirrer up of broils and discord, and to set all the members of a family at variance, like you have done ours since you came into it—does it excuse you, madam, for setting a child against its mother?"

"The mission of the Catholic Church on earth is one of peace, but it teaches that you must hear Him, who says: 'He that loves father or mother, sister or brother more than Me, is not worthy of Me.'"

"You seem to be able to adapt your religion to your own purposes; but you cannot, through it, excuse yourself to me, and I have come to demand, madam, that you go instantly to my aunt and tell her that you comply with her request."

"I have already been thrice, George, to give an explanation, and each time Aunt Caroline would not listen to anything I had to say."

"Well, if you had been a hundred times, you shall go with me now and make the promise required of you."

"I can make no promise, my husband, that conflicts with my church, which commands us to instruct the ignorant; and when Coralie, who is quite an inquisitive child, comes to me and asks if it is true that I adore pictures, statues, &c., and pay priests to forgive my sins, and if I think our Blessed

Lady equal to God, I am obliged to tell her how false and how abhorrent all these things are to a Catholic."

"And you are obliged to make peace with my aunt, or by the Eternal," he exclaimed, hitting a table near, "*you are no longer a wife of mine!*"

For an instant Mary stood looking at him in silence and wondering if this man, who so boldly and determinedly spoke of putting her away from him, could be her husband; the man she had sworn to love always, to whom she had given all the wealth of her heart, which was of infinite more value than all the worldly possessions he had bestowed upon her, and sight became dim, the room seemed to be turning rapidly around, and it was with difficulty that she could prevent herself from falling.

While this scene is being enacted, let us descend to the parlor below, where Mrs. Caroline and child, robed for a journey, are seated, the former talking rather excitedly for her, to the group around, which consists of Col. Graham, his wife, Sister Sallie, and Viola.

"Yes, she positively told me, brother, and Sister Sallie heard her, that she would imbue my child with the idolatrous doctrine of the papists, and, therefore, you must not blame me if I fly with her out of the tempter's reach."

"Leave my house! Sister Caroline, *never!*" spoke the Colonel in a voice husky with passion. "I have been master of Glen Mary since my infancy, for my father died when I was but a week old, and never yet has a guest of mine anticipated his departure, or been treated with rudeness within its hospitable walls. No! The mercenary wretch, that inveigled my son into a hasty marriage without my approval, shall be the one to go; pull the bell there, wife. Stephen," he said, addressing the servant summoned, "tell your young master to come here instantly, and to bring his wife with him."

Viola, who sat listening to this speech as long as it was possible to an impetuous nature like hers, broke out with:

"I don't care what you all think of me for interfering in your family matters. You need not roll your grey eyes in this direction, Mrs. Caroline, for I will say what I have to say, and that is, that I am surprised to see a Graham, especially Colonel Gilmore Graham, can so far forget his honor as a man, and his cultivation as a gentleman, to stoop to persecute a woman, and that woman his son's wife. Since I have been here, which was three months yesterday, she has, considering her position as the bride of your only son, and the future mistress of Glen Mary, been treated with unpardonable neglect and studied insult. What can you say now for your hospitable walls?" she added, turning towards the astonished Colonel.

At this moment Mary, pale and tottering, staggered, rather than walked, into the room, followed by her still excited husband.

The first person she saw as she entered was Sister Sallie, whose eyes shone with an exultant gleam, reminding her of the tiger as it pounces upon its prey, which had such an effect upon her that she could not speak, although she essayed to do so several times. Her silence, like everything else she had done since she become an inmate of the household, was misunderstood, and regarded by all, Viola alone excepted, as obstinacy, and a fresh insult to Mrs. Caroline. Col. Graham was so enraged that he turned to George and said:

"My son, I call upon you to choose now, and to choose forever, between me and your wife; if you take her, I and my family will accompany Sister Caroline and leave Glen Mary, but if your choice falls upon me, *she only will leave!*" pointing to Mary.

Dr. George, who was very angry, did not take time to reflect how much he would miss the gentle, loving creature that stood beside him, and whom he had vowed to love and cherish; he thought only of his father and of his kindness and indulgence to him, and, extending his hand, grasped the Colonel's, exclaiming: "My father always first."

"My son, my dear son!" exclaimed Col. Graham, as he caught him in a warm embrace.

Mrs. Col. Graham wept tears of rejoicing. Sister Sallie pathetically thanked God "that George was their own once more," whilst Mrs. Caroline looked discomfited, and Viola rushed to the assistance of Mary, who she saw was fainting, and saved her from a heavy fall. It seemed to her a long time before she could bring the poor wife back to consciousness, but she was at last rewarded with a heavy sigh, which spoke of returning animation, and the sufferer opened her eyes. Some few minutes elapsed before she recognized Viola; when she did she said:

"Viola, what is the matter? I feel that a heavy

burden is laid upon me that I cannot remove. Oh! my God, I remember now," she exclaimed as she clasped her hands in agony. "I am to be driven from my husband's home and from my husband's heart."

"Dear Mrs. Graham, do not think of that now. Col. Graham left word with me, for you, that you need not leave to-night; that in the morning the carriage will be at your service to take you wherever you please to go."

At this Mary's pale cheek flushed, but before she could speak Viola continued:

"And here is a note the Doctor left for you."

Mary caught it convulsively, and a faint smile of hope lighted up her countenance, which the first glance dispelled. It ran as follows:

"I made an irrevocable choice when I decided between you and my father, but I cannot forget that you were my wife; therefore I place at your disposal, in the Bank of B———, the sum of two thousand dollars, until the law will divorce us, and will grant you a suitable allowance to live upon.

"GEORGE GRAHAM."

Viola, who was compassionately watching her pale, sad face as she was reading the note, said: "Dear Mrs. Graham, cease to think now; let me assist you to your room, and after a good night's rest, you will feel better, and your plans will be much clearer."

"Yes, Viola, you may help me to my room, and perhaps I will feel better."

At this the kind-hearted girl threw her arms

around the suffering woman and almost carried her up the long flight of stairs which led to her chamber. At the door Mary gently dismissed her, saying:

"Viola, I will not ask you to come in; I would be alone for awhile, darling, until I can collect my scattered thoughts."

Then her conscience reproaching her for even the appearance of rudeness, she called her back and begged her not to think her unkind, saying:

"You know, my dear Viola, that you have been my only friend at Glen Mary, for which my whole heart thanks you, and it has made you very, very dear to me; and, darling, if we should never meet again, I can never forget you or cease to be grateful. Now promise me to wear this always—" handing her a small gold medal of the Immaculate Conception —"and say the prayer upon it to our Holy Mother every morning and evening of your life. Believe me, dear Viola, that it will never hurt you to ask the Mother of God to intercede in your behalf. And now good-bye, my darling, may God bless you always, and His Holy Mother and angels shield and protect you."

She kissed fondly the weeping girl, entered her room, and softly closed the door.

For a moment she stood stupefied and lost in grief, then falling on her knees, in the language of her Divine Master, she implored her Heavenly Father, that if it were possible, to let the chalice pass away from her, but that His will, not hers, be done.

After this prayer she felt both comforted and stronger, and able to collect together her small and scanty wardrobe, for she would not touch even the veriest trifle that the love or pride of Dr. Graham had invested her with. On the bureau she saw an envelope addressed to her, in her husband's handwriting. Tearing it open she found it contained a few bank notes and only these words: "For immediate use."

All hope forsook her now, and maybe, for the first time, she fully realized her forlorn condition. Clasping her hands wildly, she prayed for strength to stand this last insult.

"Oh! my God," she cried, "he has been made, too, to think that I married him only for his money, and he seeks thus to palliate his desertion of me. Mercy, my Redeemer! do not chastise too severely your poor child!"

Presently, being more composed, she walked to the window and looked out. A storm was raging outside, in keeping with the one in her own breast. It was quite dark, except when angry flashes of lightning would dart across the heavens, bringing clearly to view even the smallest object on the earth below. Heavy drops of rain were beating against the panes.

It seemed a fearful night to be a wanderer, *but she must go;* she could not breathe if she remained longer underneath the roof that had been no protection to her. For a few moments she allowed her mind to travel over the time her heart had been won by an imaginary hero. How great, how noble he appeared to her then, how happy she had been a few weeks after her marriage; secure in his love, she felt she could brave the whole world. How she had returned with him to his home, with all the love of a daughter, who had never known, but who had always longed for, a parent's love, filling her heart; how they had so cruelly given her to understand that they knew she had married their son only for his wealth. And oh! far more than all, the gradual alienation of her husband until, at last, she had become repulsive to him, and was ordered forever from his sight. Then she shuddered as she remembered a pair of brilliant, black eyes that seemed to have been haunting her all the time, and she trembled like the poor, fascinated, fluttering bird that slowly, but surely, descends into the mouth of the snake.

All this time the rain poured down and, as she leaves the house, the big, heavy drops are falling thick and fast, and continue to fall upon the weary, heart-broken woman, cast again upon the world, homeless, friendless, and alone.

"Oh! Holy Catholic Church, work of a Divine Master, in Thee, only, does woman reign a queen, and is never known as that abject thing, a cast-off wife, a divorced woman."

CHAPTER VIII.

WE are forgetting Estelle. Let us look in upon her this balmy morning, so calm after the great storm of last night, and see how it fares with her, since she has become the mistress of the grand old Abbey, which is the admiration and pride of the surrounding country.

We shall find her in the library reposing upon a crimson velvet divan, which casts a becoming shade over her clear, olive complexion, and in deep contemplation about something. What is it? She is wondering why she is not happy!

Every dream of her ambitious youth has been fulfilled. In the first place she, herself, is everything she ever wished to be, unusually gifted, accomplished in the highest degree, beautiful, almost beyond comparison, admired by all, held up as a model by mothers to their daughters, and she had unlimited control over vast wealth. Her husband she could not wish changed in the smallest particular, belonging, as he did, to the first family in the country, yet, having no near relations to trouble or annoy, possessing a bright intellect, addicted to no vice, handsome and proud. What could she wish for more? And yet, she—the beautiful and gifted Mrs. Fairfax—was not happy! And why? She turned the question over and over in her mind, and still she could not answer it.

Estelle, where was your angel guardian that he did not whisper in your ear that although you thought you possessed all, you wanted everything; and that you were poor, very poor, for you did not possess religion.

Whilst she was still pondering, her husband entered the room, attired in a hunting suit, which set off well his finely proportioned figure. Seeing Estelle, he said:

"So I have found you at last my wee wife, my darling."

"Why, I have not been playing 'hide and seek,' and there could be no difficulty in finding me if you cared to see me, which I very much doubt," she answered, petulantly.

"Indeed, I did care to see you, my precious wife," he replied, going up to her and taking her hand, "and I can convince you of the fact, for I have been looking for you all over the house to tell you that a party of hunters have arrived and have requested me to join them and to take a stand, not over a mile from here. I have promised to do so, but I could not go without telling my only one, and getting a parting kiss."

"And that, sir, you shall not get. And, what is more, you must not go, for I have no idea of staying here all morning, by myself, in this dark, gloomy old Abbey."

Mr. Fairfax looked surprised, and raised his expressive eyes in astonishment, but contrived not to let his wife see how amazed he was, as he gently spoke:

"Dear Estelle, it was very thoughtless in me to

promise to go, and not remember that you would be left alone, possibly for some hours; but, my darling, the word of a Fairfax, even in the most trivial matter, is as binding as an oath, and I am compelled to keep my promise."

"There is no compulsion about it, sir. You are not obliged to keep a promise made to a party of idlers when your wife objects, and I tell you again, once for all, that I will not spend the morning here alone."

"Then, could you not return some of the many calls you have received, Estelle, whilst I'm away?"

"Return calls by myself, ha! ha!" she said, laughing scornfully, "that would be acting the character of 'the neglected wife' to perfection. No, sir, I do not leave Dunreath Abbey to-day."

"Be careful, Estelle, be very careful how you make a Fairfax lose respect for his word, or you may never cease to regret it, for we Fairfaxes are said to be either very high or very low in the world's standard of greatness, and again I warn you that you do not make me one of the latter; but it seems that you are not to be left alone, for I see Col. Graham's carriage approaching."

"Now, sir, politeness, as well as your wife's wish, obliges you to remain, and I suppose you will have the courtesy to go with me to welcome my visitors. I do hope that Mary is one of them, for I have been anxious to see her for some days."

Here the carriage reached the door, and, after the good old fashion of the country, both the disputants went to receive their guests.

Estelle could scarcely repress a look of disappointment when she saw only the Colonel, his wife, and Mrs. Caroline descend from the carriage. When it rolled outside the enclosure she knew that Mary had not come. The greetings were soon over, and then Col. Graham spoke:

"My honor as a man, as well as my feelings as a neighbor and friend, prompted this visit. You, madam,"—addressing Estelle—"of course, have heard of the serious difficulty which occurred at Glen Mary last evening, all of which grew out of the fanaticism of your relative?"

"No, sir," answered Estelle with a puzzled countenance, "I have heard nothing, but I can well imagine that a fanatic like Mary could easily cause trouble by her constant preaching. I, myself, Colonel, have often felt the disagreeableness of her continual arguments; but tell me what it is of which you speak."

"Is it possible that Mary has not told you?"

"No, Colonel. I again repeat that I have heard nothing."

"Well, that seems strange, I had imagined that she had filled your pretty head with all sorts of prejudice against your old friend, and I almost feared a repulse when I came here this morning, but I determined to brave your displeasure, and to tell you and all the world that Col. Graham never turned a mortal outside his house on such a fearful night as last night was," said the Colonel, with vehemence.

"Oh! Colonel, tell me all about it; I am all ears," replied Estelle, now really alarmed.

"Well, to begin at the beginning. In the first place, I was very much opposed to my son, my only son, marrying a Romanist, for I was afraid that some of the heathenish doctrines of that old church might creep into my house and into my family. My boy argued that we could avoid contamination, as he would prohibit his wife ever mentioning her belief, and in a moment of weakness I consented. The instant I did so I would have given worlds to recall it, but as no excuse offered itself, I was obliged to see George immolated, and from that time to this have never ceased to mourn the sacrifice, for truly she was a breeder of discord in my once happy family."

At this Estelle's cheek flushed crimson, and she hastily interrupted him with:

"Be more choice, Col. Graham, in the words you use, for in Dunreath Abbey, Mary shall not be defamed."

"Pardon, madam, if I have offended, but the relation that Mary still holds to me, being my son's wife, will excuse the force with which I have spoken. As I was going on to say, last evening she deliberately informed my sister there," pointing towards Mrs. Caroline, who instantly raised a pretty piece of lace to her eyes, that she would teach her child the doctrine of her Church, and tried to excuse her insolence by saying it was her duty to do so. My sister could not stand this, so she resorted to the most lady-like course she could pursue, which was to remove her child from the Glen. This, I would not allow, so we tried persuasion and entreaty to induce your cousin not to tamper with Coralie, but without the slightest effect; and, at last, when we had done everything that could be done, I required my son to choose between me and his wife—that if he sided with her, I and my wife would leave with Caroline; but if he preferred me, Mary only should leave. My dear boy," here the Colonel wiped a tear from his cheek, "would not give up his grey-haired old father, which, Mrs. Mary seeing, she takes herself off, on such a night as last night was, to make the world and you, madam, think that I was an unfeeling monster to send a young woman adrift in such a fearful tempest."

"Oh! where did she go? Where is she?" cried Estelle in affright.

"Why, is she not here?" exclaimed the Colonel and Mrs. Caroline in equal consternation, whilst Mrs. Graham looked as if she did not know what to do, but gave a sigh of relief as she determined to await the effect Mary's not being there would have upon the Colonel.

"On my honor, my dear madam, we thought she was over here, or we would have had the entire neighborhood searched long ere this," explained Col. Graham in great excitement.

Up to this time Mr. Fairfax had not spoken, so intent was he upon every word that was being uttered. Now he advanced quickly to Col. Graham's side and, in a low voice, tremulous with emotion, said:

"Sir, if it were not for your grey hairs, I would

hold you responsible for your son's wife, for her being a wanderer, and homeless on any night, particularly on such a night as last night was. You are too old a man; but, thank heaven, you have a son, and that son shall account to me for my wife's only relative being roofless last night."

There was a tone of stern resolve in his voice and a look of unflinching determination in his face, that made the old man quail before him—for Col. Graham did quail if danger threatened his child, and this was considered his only weakness—whilst both the Mrs. Grahams changed color.

"No, no, Alfred, my friend, do not make any threats or resolve on vengeance; for poor George, who is absent from home, does not know that his wife stole away in the night. We came over, thinking she was here, with the intention of taking her back to him, if she would go on our conditions."

"On your conditions! Have you never thought, old man, that you are persecuting Mary Graham? If you have not, I can tell you that others have, and her pale cheeks and languid eyes have told them so for many weeks."

"Stop, stop all this talk!" interposed Mrs. Col. Graham, as she was about to advance an idea for the first time in her life—but what cannot a mother do to save her offspring! "Whilst you are all wrangling here, the poor child may be suffering, somewhere, from cold and exposure. Your duty, husband, as the father of Mary, is to hunt her up, and yours, Mr. Fairfax, is to assist in the search, as she is your relative also. But promise me, gentlemen, before I order my carriage, that all disputes will cease until the child is found. Her not being here seems serious. Do you promise me, gentlemen?" At this point the lady shed tears, and what will not a woman's tears effect? Both the men pledged their honor to keep the peace till the absent one was recovered, and immediate preparations were made to begin the search.

Estelle, no longer objecting to be left alone, insisted upon her husband accompanying the party to Glen Mary, as all wisely concluded that it was better to commence the hunt at the place she was last seen.

CHAPTER IX.

WE have purposely refrained from locating the scene of our story, for fear the life history which it contains might open afresh wounds which, we trust, have long since been closed. But for the better understanding of our readers, we will have to go back to the usual beginning of a history, and give the topography of the country where the occurrences we are about to narrate took place, though, fortunately, the description answers to so many other places in the Atlantic States of America, that we hope the little geography we are obliged to give will not indicate the locality, and thus give pain to some of the actors.

Glen Mary was situated far off in the mountains of one of the seaboard states. Its name was derived from Col. Graham's grandmother, Mary, and from the pretty glen in which it was located, as well as from the associations connected with the great poet, whom the Colonel's ancestors were proud to claim as countryman.

Scottish remembrances and the love of Scotland also named Dunreath Abbey

Lovely dells, murmuring brooks, vast mountains, and musical rivers were to be seen, far and near, for many miles in every direction from those two grand old homesteads; and no wonder the inhabitants shuddered when they thought of Mary wandering alone and in darkness through such a country.

Whoever beheld the grandeur, the beauty, the majesty of mountain scenery without being impressed with the almighty power of Nature's great Architect who, out of nothing, has given us, as it were, a glimpse of His immensity, and without a feeling of the awfulness of God's greatness creeping over him? And if the heavens should lend their artillery to reverberate among the hundred hills, to encircle them here and there like an angry, fiery serpent with its vivid flashes of light, raising the gentle rivers into dashing torrents, and bringing out all the sublimity of the lofty mountains by the clouds hanging upon their brows, concealing their crests, does he not feel himself sink into utter insignificance, by the side of that terrible magnificence and incomprehensibility of the Creator? Surely it was wisely said that the man who saith in his own heart that there is no God, is a fool.

Thoughts similar to these passed through the mind of Dr. George Graham as, late in the evening, we last saw him. He was riding rapidly anywhere, anywhere to escape from the remembrance of his wronged wife. He had turned a sharp angle in the road, when the view just pictured, in all its transcendent beauty, burst suddenly upon him, and so terribly grand did it appear, that even the crazy rider paused in awe and admiration to look upon it, forgetting for awhile the storm which raged within his own breast. His lethe lasted only a few short moments, when he again urged his steed on at the same rapid gait, not knowing, not caring what path he followed. Hour after hour he rode in this manner, never once thinking of the torture he was inflicting upon the poor, obedient brute that carried him. He could not stop, for everywhere he turned, the gentle, patient face of Mary was looking reproachfully at him, and he must escape it. Would it never go away, and would he never be at rest again?

"No, never, never," thus he soliloquized, and still went on, until his exhausted horse gave a lurch forward and fell to the ground, dead. The sudden end of the rapid ride caused the rider a heavy fall, and he lay for some moments insensible. When he recovered he was completely bewildered, and it was a long time before remembrance was added to consciousness. At last, after many vain efforts to recollect, he knew where he was and what it was that caused him so much pain.

He was suffering both mentally and physically, for, when he raised up and tried to throw his arms around the neck of the faithful animal he had so cruelly killed, he found his left arm was broken above the elbow, causing him exquisite suffering. With a groan he laid back, and at that moment what would he not have given for the loving wife he had driven from him to mesmerize the pain from his throbbing temple with the gentle pressure of her small, soft hand. As he wished for her, he went over in thought the few months that she had been his; her patience, her sweetness, her love, all rose up before him, and sent a thrill of agony to his inmost heart.

Oh! if he could think of something, no matter how slight the cause, that could justify, even in the smallest degree, his cruelty, he would feel more composed. But no, no, there was no flaw to be found in the lovely character of his pure, young wife. And then, as the remembrance of her poor, pale face came back once more, as he last saw it, resting on Viola's shoulder, a cry of pain escaped him, and he determined not to give her up.

"My darling, my precious one, you shall not go away from me! No father, no mother, no earthly being shall separate us! I will go back this instant and, on my knees, implore your forgiveness and plead, with all the earnestness of my soul, till you take me to your heart again."

This resolve removed a weight of grief from him, and, in spite of his fractured arm, he sprang lightly to his feet and commenced his homeward walk, but not before taking an affectionate and sad farewell of the noble horse whose life was lost in obedience to his will.

As he started he remembered that it was raining, and that a fearful tempest was raging. The earth was so thoroughly saturated with water that it was with difficulty he could walk at all; and the loud and frightful thunder which he, for the first time noticed, added to the terribleness of the storm.

Flash after flash of vivid lightning followed in quick succession, and almost blinded him, but still he persevered and went on. True, he had many miles to walk, over rugged mountains, through lonesome valleys, dark and dangerous woods, but what did that matter? Was he not returning to Mary to sue forgiveness, and would she not smile upon and pity him, when she saw his fatigue, his suffering, and his repentance? Yes! he knew she needed but one word to be his own loving wife once more. He thought not of the difficulty of the path he followed. His mind, his brain, his heart, were filled but with one idea, and that was Mary.

For hours he walked on, never faltering, never weary; on the contrary, his speed increased as he approached nearer to where she was. But at length an obstacle bars his progress, and he is forced to stop. One of the many rivers in the country has risen far above high water mark, and the usual placid stream is now a raging torrent. It were certain death to attempt to ford it, and nothing but this knowledge could have stopped the young man on his rapid journey. The war of its mad waters drowned the loud voice of the thunder as they fiercely dashed onward to the sea. George, completely disheartened, turned, not knowing what to do.

Just at this instant, a long, bright flash brought each indistinct object plainly to view, and he saw before him, immediately in his path, the white, startled face of a woman, and that woman his wife! With a loud shriek he rushed away, and went on, on, until exhausted nature could stand no more, and he fell to the ground, the second time, unconscious.

* * * * *

Scarcely had Col. Graham and party returned from Dunreath Abbey, when they saw a man approaching them on horseback.

The Colonel, recognizing the servant he had sent in quest of his young master, who was still unaccountably absent, rose hurriedly to his feet and went to meet him. In answer to his master's enquiries, "Where is my son, and what is the matter?" the man asked the Colonel to walk aside and, in a low voice, told him that he had traced the Doctor to the nearest town, and that there he was told, after depositing some money in the bank for his wife, that, in spite of the expostulations of friends, and many prophesies that it was suicide to ride in such a storm, that he mounted his horse and rode at breakneck speed in the exact opposite direction to his home.

"And, sir," went on the servant, "I took the road they pointed out, and followed it for many miles, until my horse refused to go further. I then got down from him, tied him to a tree, and walked on in the hope of either overtaking my young master, or meeting him upon his return. I walked until I had got so tired I thought I would have to give up the search, when I saw something dark lying to the left of me, that I could not account for. I went over to it, and no one knows how I felt, sir, when I saw master George's favorite horse Terror stiff and dead. When I got over my surprise, I began to look around me, and could see, here and there, my young master's footprints in the mud. I followed them, mile after mile, until, sir ——"

"Until what?" cried the excited Colonel, as the man paused.

"Until, sir, they brought me to the very brink of K—— River, which is even now impossible to cross."

"My God! my God! You do not think my son drowned, do you?"

"I don't know, sir; but this I do know, that if he went into that water, he could not live, and his footprints lead right to the river's brink."

Here the Colonel reeled and would have fallen, but for Mr. Fairfax, who sprang forward to support him.

All now was the wildest confusion at the Glen, for the servant soon made the others acquainted with what his master already knew, and the poor mother was carried to her room in hysterics, and now, when for the first time she needed sympathy and condolence, there were none to give it to her. All were taken up with their own thoughts about the information they had just received, and Sister Sallie was administering relief to the Colonel.

Mr. Fairfax waited until the Colonel was brought back to consciousness, and then, collecting all the able-bodied men on the place, he instituted a search for the missing man, which resulted in his being brought home that evening in a state of delirium and excitement, bordering on actual madness.

CHAPTER X.

SO great was the anxiety about Glen Mary's young heir, that, for a time, Mary was forgotten, save by Viola, Coralie, and some of the servants, who often thought of her consideration for them, and wondered amongst themselves, what could have become of their gentle mistress.

Although three weeks have passed forever away since Dr. Graham was carried home in a senseless condition, his attendants are still uncertain whether life or death will claim him. He is still lingering between the two, now leaning towards one, then towards the other, until his idolizing parents are almost distracted with the alternations of hope and despair. Let us enter the sick room with the physician now going in, and view the sufferer for ourselves.

We can scarcely recognize, in the emaciated form before us, with those wild, rolling eyes and bright, feverish cheeks, the person of Dr. George Graham, whom lately we saw in all the vigor of health and strength.

We involuntarily glance towards the physician to know if there is hope; but that sage individual will only shake his head with a slow, solemn motion, raising his eyes ceilingward, looking unutterable things, and slowly articulate "a doubtful case, a very doubtful case." Nothing more can be gotten from this son of Æsculapius, so we must content ourselves with our own opinion, and fear we will have to agree with him in thinking it a very doubtful case.

Ah! the sick man moves, and his poor, feverish lips utter a word which they keep repeating, louder and louder each time, until the name of Mary is borne in a shriek upon the air, and his bright eyes wander from object to object in an impatient search for something, or somebody.

The Doctor paces to and fro during his patient's excitement, which, at first, he hopes will be only transitory; but as it increases, until its fearfulness makes the attendants shudder, he administers a strong nervine and, when he sees the sick man under its control, he, for the first time, speaks:

"Col. Graham, you must confide in me, and tell me who and what this Mary is your son is continually calling, for unless I know the cause of his illness, which, with the exception of a slight fracture in the arm, is entirely a mental one, I cannot promise you to save his life. Do not imagine that I wish to pry into your family matters. I have no more curiosity than this stick has, which I hold; but I must know the cause of this unusual excitement, or I give up the case."

"Oh! Dr. Fitzpatrick," exclaimed both the father and mother, "do not talk of abandoning our child. We have more faith in you than in the whole medical faculty of the state, and you shall possess our entire confidence."

They then gave the physician a minute account of George's marriage, which occurred during Dr. Fitzpatrick's absence on the Continent, and graphically told of all the unhappiness which resulted from it, and finally the separation, coloring it all with the light in which they viewed it, and feeling themselves fully justified in trying to excite some of the good Doctor's sympathy in behalf of their child, as they pathetically dwelt upon his many wrongs.

The physician waited patiently until all was told, only interrupting the narrative with an occasional grunt, or a slight tap on his gold headed cane, and then abruptly asked:

"Where can Mrs. Graham be found?"

To this question no satisfactory answer could be given, when the now excited Doctor said:

"My God! You can't mean to tell me that you never hunted up the poor, young creature you sent out into the pitiless storm of that dreadful night?"

"There is our excuse, sir," answered the Colonel, pointing to his sick son.

"And there," replied the Doctor, pointing also to the sick man, "is a life depending upon her being found."

"Oh! Dr. Fitzpatrick, you don't mean to tell us——"

"I mean to tell you this, that until your son's eyes rest upon the form of his wife, the wild delirium that has overthrown his reason, and which I fear is hurrying him to his grave, cannot be subdued."

"What shall we do! what shall we do to find her? Direct us, Doctor. Our minds are too much troubled to think or act for ourselves," exclaimed Col. Graham, almost in a frenzy.

"I am afraid, sir, that you have lost precious time. You should have confided in me before; but if I were in your place, Colonel, I would send at once to her relatives, the Fairfaxes, and ascertain if they have learned anything of her whereabouts.'

"I thank you, Doctor, for the suggestion, and will send at once."

The Colonel wrote a hurried note and left the room. The servant dispatched with it, soon returned with the following answer:

"COLONEL GILMORE GRAHAM.

"*Sir:*—I have left no means untried, since I last saw you, to find my wife's cousin, but, unfortunately, have not met with even the shadow of success. The matter has been placed in the hands of the ablest police, and the best detectives throughout the state, but no person answering to the description of Mrs. Graham has been seen. I have given up all hope, and believe that the cruelty that drove my fair relative from the protection of home, during such an awful storm, has also driven her to a premature grave. I am making preparations to drag the rivers this morning to recover her body.

"Respectfully,
"ALFRED FAIRFAX.
"*Dunreath Abbey, July 10th, 18—.*"

After this unsatisfactory note was read, a long silence followed, and a feeling of despair seemed to have fallen upon all present, which was, at last, broken by the Colonel, who cried out:

"For God's sake tell me, Dr. Fitzpatrick, what I must do to save my child?"

"In the first place, Col. Graham, I would send assistance to young Fairfax, to help drag the rivers, for, perhaps after all, he may be mistaken in the dreadful conclusion he has arrived at. Then, if the body is not found, I would advertise for her all over the country, and insert in the advertisement that she is summoned to the deathbed of her husband. That will bring her if nothing else will."

"But in the meantime, sir, what can we do for George?"

"We must resort to strategy."

"Strategy! What do you mean?"

"Why, I mean that we must dress some woman, like her in size and appearance, in some of your daughter-in-law's clothes—I presume that she did not take all she had away with her—and in Dr. Graham's darkened chamber we may, by forbidding speech, make him believe that she is really present, and his driving her from him but one of the many hallucinations of his fever. Do you know of any one that resembles her?"

"Oh! Viola does, for we have often remarked the unaccountable likeness between them, a likeness which is seldom seen in perfect strangers," exclaimed Mrs. Graham. Then, turning to Viola, she asked:

"Viola, will you not assist us?"

"You forget, Mrs. Graham," the young girl answered, "that I have not Mary's gentle manner or soft speech, and it would be hard to deceive Dr. Graham, when his nervous condition would make him fully alive to the turning over of chairs, breaking of bottles, my loud voice, &c."

At this ingenious answer, Dr. Fitzpatrick could not repress a smile as he spoke:

"Miss Viola, you are not expected to create confusion, or to use any of your oratorical powers, but simply to be seated in the room in such a position that, when the crisis of the disease, which is near at hand now, I think, is reached, and consciousness—which is usually given the patient at that time—returns, his eyes may rest on you, and thus become convinced, in his own mind, that his wife is alive and near him. He will then, I trust, sink into a natural sleep, and when he awakes and calls for you, I will tell him that I have forbidden you the room—you know we doctors are privileged characters—and whilst he may think me unnecessarily precautious, the impression that he has seen his wife alive and well cannot be erased from his mind."

"But when he is well and strong, and dear Mary is not here—" commenced Viola with quivering lips and eyes full of tears, which prevented her finishing the sentence

"Then I will manage him, and take all the responsibility off of you; but"—in a softened voice which showed he had noticed the girl's agitation—"let us hope by that time she will be here."

"God grant it," Viola replied, as she left the room to prepare to reappear as Mary.

Dr. Fitzpatrick followed her, and continued gazing in the direction she took, apparently hoping to see her again. Waiting, in vain, for some moments, he turned to Col. Graham and asked if that young lady was a relative of the family, at the same time remarking that she displayed fine sensibilities, and he thought her rather a superior person.

"She is no relative," quickly replied Sister Sallie, who was seated opposite the Doctor, and upon whom his wistful gaze after Viola was not lost.

"Well, who is she?" persisted Dr. Fitzpatrick, who did not like the tone in which "she is no relative" was said.

"She is a friend, or rather her mother is, of Caroline's, and Mrs. Williams has placed Viola under sister's charge, in the hope that she will be able to infuse some of her refinement of manner and delicacy of feeling into this wild creature."

"Humph!" grunted the Doctor; "delicacy of feeling, indeed. That means, I suppose, that she is to be robbed of all natural outbursts of affection, and turned, from a warm-hearted, impulsive girl, into an icicle; or, in other words, changed into a cold, dignified, feelingless woman of the world."

"I think you are rather severe on poor Mrs. Williams," replied the charitable Sallie; "for if Viola was the warm-hearted girl you think her, she would never have left a widowed, invalid mother to be nursed by strangers, suffering in an unhealthy city for one breath of the pure air of our mountains, which Viola does not at all need.

"Dear Mrs. Williams," she sighed. "When I think of all her unselfishness, and the love which she has wasted upon this thoughtless, unfeeling girl, it nearly breaks my heart," and the lady touchingly concealed her face in her handkerchief.

When Viola reached her room there was a strange

flutter at her heart, and a glance at the mirror opposite showed there was an unusual amount of color on either cheek. She asked herself the cause, knowing beforehand that she would never answer the question, and willing to attribute it to anything else than the true one—that the great and good man, Dr. Fitzpatrick, had kindly noticed and looked with approval, if not with a stronger feeling, upon her—her, whom every person was inclined to lecture and find fault with.

Try as she might to please, she never succeeded; not even with her suffering mother, who drove her from her because she could not stand her heedless, careless ways. Oh! why was she so unfortunate, so different from other people? She did not mean to be so, and yet she was, for even an impartial mother noticed the difference. There never was but one person who seemed to be able to endure her, and that was the patient, gentle Mary.

As she thought of Mary, she remembered for the first time the medal and the prayer she was told to say. Sinking on her knees, she asked, with all the fervor of a poor, young, wounded heart, the Mother of Love to love her, to guide and direct her, and in childlike language asked her to make her good.

It is a dreadful thing to be misunderstood by those we love—try as we will to make ourselves known and loved by them, and to feel that all our efforts only increase their distrust of us. How many such unfortunates there are in this world of ours, which God has made so bright and beautiful and man has made so hard and miserable.

If we are blessed with the true religion, we do not care even if we are unjustly dealt with, for we can unite our sufferings with the injustice our Saviour bore with such loving fortitude for us, feeling happy in being able to suffer something for Him, consoled by the promised blessing to all those who are reviled and persecuted; but if, like Viola, we are deprived of the truth, that blessed truth that has a balm for every wound the heart can receive, then we are truly miserable if we pour out the wealth of our hearts upon creatures, and receive nothing but coldness, indifference, and fault-finding.

Viola arose from her knees refreshed and strengthened, feeling that she had now a Mother whom she would be allowed to love, and who would both love and protect her. She hastily dressed herself in Mary's clothes, and was startled at the strong resemblance between them.

When she returned to the invalid's chamber, she felt every eye was upon her except the pair she had eagerly sought for, and she felt both pained and mortified when he coolly pointed towards the seat she was to take, without even so much as a glance, and for the remainder of the evening seemed entirely oblivious of her presence.

Our pen refuses to describe the agonizing suspense of the poor father and mother, whose only child's life lay literally hanging by a thread. Suffice it to say, the ruse succeeded, and from the deep, heavy sleep which followed the return of consciousness, those two weary watchers were told by the man of medicine "to hope for the best."

CHAPTER XI.

THERE are some persons in this world that love to stab; they do not handle the poniards or light stilettoes used by the Roman ladies of old, but they use much smaller weapons which inflict deeper, and ofttimes more incurable wounds, than the bright steel already mentioned. The names of those weapons are covetousness, maliciousness, and heartlessness, and the name of one of the persons using them is Mrs. Sallie Graham, better known as "Sister Sallie." She possessed all three of these deadly instruments, and used them most skilfully, the more so because they were concealed, and those she stabbed were always ignorant of the hand that inflicted the wound; for who would have suspected in that dignified, quiet lady, a heartless, vindictive woman who lived only for self, and who, to accomplish her ends, would as freely trample lives beneath her feet as we would the dust of the street.

In early life she was subjected to many hard trials. Her father, the only remaining relative she had, ran through an immense fortune by dissipation and card playing, and left her an orphan, dependent upon charity, before she had attained her nineteenth year. For two years she struggled desperately with the world, with one object only in view, and which she never, for an instant, lost sight of. It was to marry for station and wealth, and thus secure to herself again what her father had deprived her of.

"Where there is a will, there is a way" was true in her case, and at twenty-one, she was married to the wealthiest and most distinguished lawyer in the country, and she became at once the acknowledged leader and belle of society.

It is needless to say that a woman whose sole object in marriage was wealth, did not love her husband. We suspect that she never once asked herself the question. She loved, it is true, but she loved his money, not him.

It was far otherwise with Mr. Graham. He fairly idolized his handsome, young wife, and thought, at first, his affection was returned with all its ardor, and he would have deemed it a suspicion, unworthy of her, not so to think; but as gradually the truth burst upon him in its full force, and he realized that this beautiful, fascinating creature loved him not, and was both cold and mercenary, his health, which was always delicate, rapidly gave way, and, in less than a year afterwards, he went to sleep, and dreamed of his lovely wife no more.

During the time of his illness Mrs. Graham appeared to the world, and especially to the afflicted Colonel, as the personification of all that was good, gentle, and devoted.

After he was laid in the tomb she was taken to Glen Mary, where she now reigned the acknowledged mistress, which position she determined, with all the force of her strong character, to maintain. She has one more secret—lean nearer, reader, whilst we tell you, for it must be told in a whisper, and remember you are never to repeat it. *She is in love with Dr. Fitzpatrick*, and has resolved to bring him to her feet.

Dr. Graham regained his health and strength much more rapidly than could possibly have been hoped, even by those who were the most anxious for his recovery. In two weeks from the time we last saw him, he was declared convalescent, and was able to have his lounge drawn out on the balcony that overlooked the prettiest of all the beautiful views that could be seen, in every direction, from Glen Mary. One evening he was lounging there and, invalid fashion, ever using his prerogative to grumble as much as he pleased, when Mrs. Graham, who never left him a moment, gently remonstrated.

"Well, mother, what else could you expect from me?" he replied querulously.

"What else expect?" interposed Dr. Fitzpatrick. "Why, we could expect that a young man, in all the bloom of youth, and health, and strength, and with everything to live for, who, suddenly and unexpectedly tottered upon the brink of the grave, from which only a kind Providence could snatch him, would be grateful for his rescue, instead of showing dissatisfaction and displeasure every instant."

The deep, solemn tones of voice in which this rebuke was uttered, caused a momentary silence, when the invalid again spoke:

"It is very easy for a light heart to remonstrate with a heavy one. Suppose, Dr. Fitzpatrick, you put yourself in my place," he added with a bitter smile. "Imagine yourself married to a woman you love, and then imagine yourself sick unto death, and know and feel yourself deserted by the wife of your heart; could you then be so very thankful and admirably patient, as you would have me be?"

"Have I not told you repeatedly, George, that your wife could not come to you?"

"Why not, pray? Do you suppose that if she was sick, like I am, and wanted me, that I would let all the doctors in the world prevent my going to her?"

"I hope not, George."

"Then have I not cause for complaint, when she allows only one to keep her away from me? Stop, Dr. Fitzpatrick, I am a physician as well as yourself, sir, and I know that the presence of Mary, instead of retarding my recovery, would promote it."

"For once physicians agree," exclaimed Dr. Fitzpatrick, "and would to God your beautiful young wife were here to aid in your recovery."

The Colonel and the Mrs. Colonel started and looked at the speaker as if they thought he had lost his senses, whilst George rapidly glanced from one to the other of the group surrounding him, and seemed to be slowly taking in the full horror of the words he had just heard.

"My dear George," continued the Doctor, "it is time now for you to be fully undeceived, and to know that upon you depends entirely the recovery of Mary. Be a man, and cease wasting your strength in idle complaints, whilst the woman you vowed before God to protect and cherish, is a homeless wanderer."

With a deep groan the sick man fell back upon his couch, and a silence of some fifteen minutes followed. Then George asked to be enlightened as to every particular concerning the means tried to bring home the wanderer. They kindly and gently told him all, and finished by saying: "That there was no longer any fear of her having been lost during that fearful storm, as all the rivers had been carefully dragged, and the whole country diligently searched. For many miles around, in every direction, the people had been notified, and no person answering to Mary's description had been found dead, and from these facts they hoped that she had not perished, and was then with some of her childhood friends."

"And no such person answering to her description has been found alive," bitterly answered the husband. "Oh! my wife! my poor, wronged wife, where are you? And it was your sweet, pale face that I saw by the river, and, fool that I was, knew you not, and left you, perhaps to perish."

Here, seeing that words were inadeqaute to quell the tempest that raged within the suffering Doctor's breast, Dr. Fitzpatrick forced him to take a strong nervine, which shortly afterwards caused him to slumber. After this, his recovery was very rapid; feeling now the necessity of strength, his strong desire for it seemed to give it to him, and it was not long until he was dismissed by his physician as a well man.

When he was just able to take a few steps, he asked to be assisted into Mary's room, and the first thing he saw on his entrance, was the cruel note he had written his wife on that never-to-be-forgotten evening when he drove her from him. He took it up, glanced at its contents, tore it to atoms, which he ground with his heel, as if anxious to destroy the remotest particle of his cruelty. He then hastily surveyed the apartment and soon saw that all the costly gifts, which he had so lavishly bestowed upon his wife, in those first happy weeks after their marriage, were returned to him.

He gave a sigh of relief when he remembered the check he had sent her, and which, he trusted was yet keeping her from want. An idea struck him. She could not have drawn the check the night she left; she must have done it afterwards. Here was a certain way of finding out if she had survived the storm.

He wrote a hasty note to the bank, dispatched a servant, with the order not to save horse flesh, and waited impatiently till the two hours were over, which would be the shortest time the messenger could return on. At the end of the time specified, he was seen approaching rapidly, and handed his master the following note:

"DR. GEORGE GRAHAM.

"*Dear Sir:*—The money deposited here for your wife's benefit has never been drawn, and no person answering to the description you sent us has been seen in our town.

"Respectfully,
"H. R. BAKER.

"B——, *August* 2d, 18—."

A cry of affright escaped the poor watchful mother, as she saw the anguish depicted upon the emaciated face of her son as he read.

"What is it, my boy?" she kindly asked, as she drew his head gently upon her breast.

In answer, he handed her the note. After reading it she said:

"Well, child, I see nothing here to cause you such distress."

"Nothing, mother; *nothing!*" he repeated in a voice that made her shudder. "Is it nothing that my wife, even if alive, is a homeless beggar? O my God, my God! this is more than I can bear."

CHAPTER XII.

MRS. Caroline was still a guest at Glen Mary, and had determined not to leave until she saw peace and harmony restored to its once happy halls.

Coralie and Viola were thrown much together, as they were both forbidden the sick chamber, and they delighted in taking long rambles over the hills and mountains that surrounded the Glen, occasionally culling a flower and stopping to view the beauties of the natural growth of these forest hills. Another favorite amusement was boating on a stream that wound its way through the lovely valley in which Glen Mary reposed. The summer before Viola had taken lessons in rowing, and now she was an expert in rapidly gliding the little skiff that Col. Graham had caused to be made for the two children, as he called them, although Viola was nearing her nineteenth year.

On the evening already referred to, when George was made acquainted with the dreadful truth that his wife's absence was not an hallucination, but a sad reality, the two girls were seen approaching the Glen, from the balcony, by Sister Sallie, Mrs. Caroline, and Dr. Fitzpatrick, who were seated there, and who stayed for some hours after the anxious parents had carried their sick boy to his room.

Mrs. Caroline was gently reprimanding the Doctor for his abrupt disclosure to George, which he was receiving with a quiet smile that somewhat puzzled his lecturer, when the children came up. Viola's hat, together with many stray ringlets, were lying carelessly upon her neck and shoulders, her face was flushed from exercise, and her eyes had an unusual amount of brightness, as she commenced to give the particulars of their boating excursion to Coralie's mother. The man of science present thought he had never gazed upon a lovelier picture, and was forcibly reminded of the lines:

> "Ne'er did Grecian chisel trace,
> A nymph, a naiad, or a grace,
> With finer form, or lovelier face."

Sister Sallie caught his look of admiration, and turned to her sister-in-law to ask:

"Carrie, have you never thought of the extreme danger of these boating excursions?"

"Thought of danger? No, never. Why, Viola constantly assures me there is none whatever."

"Ha! ha!" laughed sweetly the sister in reply. "Is Viola your only authority? Why, Carrie, I thought you knew her want of candor, where her pleasure is concerned, better than to allow her to endanger the life of your child."

At this unexpected and unprovoked attack, the roses on Viola's cheeks were imparted to brow and neck, her eyes flashed, and her voice trembled as she attempted to vindicate herself, which she did without noticing the rude speech of Mrs. Sallie.

"Mrs. Graham, you will not believe that I would heedlessly endanger Coralie? I know that you will not, and I know that you will believe me when I tell you that there is no danger in our boating."

"Oh! no, not a particle of danger," sarcastically interrupted Sallie, "though you might row your boat over the fall, just below where you cross, which is only forty feet, and then your light skiff might spring aleak, taking you with it to the bottom of the river; but still there would be no danger, none whatever, to the 'Lady of the Lake,' which character, I understand, you are trying to assume."

Not even this ill-natured speech, which was devoid of all truthfulness, called forth a reply from Viola. This heedless girl seemed to have penetration enough to divine the attack made upon her, and plainly saw that her antagonist was anxious to cause her to display her temper in the presence of Dr. Fitzpatrick, whilst she herself preserved her lady-like demeanor.

Mrs. Caroline's cheeks paled as she thought of the danger her child had escaped, and, drawing Coralie towards her, she clasped her in her arms as though she was about to lose her forever. "My darling, I knew not before the danger you were in." Then, turning towards Sallie, she said in a voice tremulous with emotion:

"Dear sister, what could I do without you; and how can I ever sufficiently thank you for all you have done for me? You first saved my Coralie's soul, and now her body."

This was the additional straw that broke the camel's back. Viola, who would not fight for herself, could not stand this unkind allusion to Mary. The flush which, up to this time, dyed her face crimson, entirely forsook it, leaving it deadly pale. Her hand, which clasped the railing for support, trembled so she could hold it no longer, and she was the personification of a beautiful fury as she exclaimed :

"You! you, Mrs. Graham! You can thank that arch-hypocrite there," pointing to Sister Sallie, "for turning the gentlest, the sweetest, and the best woman in the world out at night to perish. And you think she did it to save your child from harm? Then let me enlighten you and tell you why it was done. She foully and maliciously manufactured stories to injure the young wife that came amongst you, and claimed your protection, to establish more firmly her rule at Glen Mary, which she feared the rightful mistress would weaken, or perhaps destroy."

Here the excited girl stopped for want of breath, whilst the astonished listeners gazed upon her in surprise, none more so than the woman whose conscience told her she had been read aright.

Mrs. Caroline was the first to recover herself, and, in a low, stern voice, ordered Viola to apologize, or to go instantly to her room, and there remain until she had retracted every insulting accusation she had uttered against Sallie.

A smile of cool contempt curled the girl's lips as she replied :

"I am no longer a child, Mrs. Graham, nor will I be ordered as one."

"Do you refuse to obey me, miss? Then I will send you back immediately to your mother, with the word that you are incorrigible."

This determination had the effect of bringing Viola to her senses. She sprang forward and caught Mrs. Caroline's hand in both of hers, saying:

"Oh! Mrs. Graham, do not do that. Do not pain my poor, sick mother. I will do whatever you wish me to, except—except retract what I have said. That, with truth, I cannot; but I am sorry now I have said it, and will tell your sister so."

Here the sister interposed.

"I do not wish you to tell me anything, Miss Williams. I hope," smiling sweetly, "Sister Caroline, you do not think that I at all mind what an angry girl will say? I am afraid that Dr. Fitzpatrick is tired of the scene she is trying to create, so you had better dismiss her, and let us resume our former conversation."

Mrs. Graham arose, took the hand of each of the girls, and lead them away to a summer-house near, where she, in her usual manner, expostulated with Viola upon her rudeness and temper, ending the lecture by positively prohibiting boating excursions in the future.

Coralie followed her mother out, and left Viola, ashamed and weeping, with her head bowed upon her arms, and vainly trying to assist her better nature to conquer in the strife that was going on within. At last she remembered her medal, and, sinking upon her knees, she implored her Heavenly Mother to aid her, and again, in her childlike manner, asked her to pray for her that she might be good.

"My poor child, do you then feel so very bad?" said a soft voice near her, whilst a hand was gently laid upon her head.

She looks up and, with an exclamation of surprise, starts to her feet.

"Oh! Dr. Fitzpatrick, are you here?"

"Yes. As I was passing by I saw your distress, and stopped to offer you a word of comfort."

"And what can you say that will comfort me, after I have behaved so badly this evening, and caused so much pain to my guardian?"

"Why, my child, I can tell you not to despair, and that you will not be rejected by our Father in Heaven if, with true penitence, you ask his forgiveness, and promise never to offend again."

"Oh! Doctor, I have done that so often, and broken my promise every time."

"Well, even if you have been so unfortunate, He who has commanded us to forgive our brothers seventy times seven, will be more patient with His poor, weak children, than we can possibly be with each other."

"I never thought of that before. That is a beautiful thought, Dr. Fitzpatrick, and I thank you for it," said the young girl with enthusiasm. Then looking suddenly up in his face, she added:

"I wish I was good like you are, sir."

The Doctor smiled and replied: "Don't you know to whom much is given, much is required? I have been blessed with the true religion since I was a child at my mother's knee, whilst you, poor lamb,

I imagine, were left to wander, without the fold, whithersoever you pleased."

"Yes, that is true, but is it too late, or am I too bad to be admitted into that fold, sir?"

"'Other sheep have I, which are not of My Fold; them will I also bring, and there shall be but one Fold and one Shepherd.' Don't you remember?" he asked, bending forward.

"Yes, sir, but could I be one of those sheep?"

"Why not, child, are you not invited by our good, kind Lord to come to Him, and He will refresh you, and make you His own?"

"Oh! but how must I go?"

"Go, child, by lifting up your heart to Him, or as He tells you, 'Ask, and it shall be given you; seek, and you shall find; knock, and it shall be opened to you,' and by obeying His first and greatest commandment, which tells you to love Him with thy whole heart, with thy whole soul, with all thy strength, and with all thy mind; and then adds, 'You must love thy neighbor as thyself.' And remember, Viola, that St. Paul says: 'Mankind of every description is your neighbor,' *even*," here he let his voice sink to a whisper, "*Mrs. Sallie Graham.*"

The girl started and hid her face in her hands with a very perceptible shudder, which made Dr. Fitzpatrick sigh as he walked away, to think how much this poor child had to overcome of self, before she could be what she so ardently wished to become, namely: A true follower of Christ.

CHAPTER XIII.

WE have left Estelle for a long time. We must now return to her for a while, though we fear our visit will not be pleasant, as she has not yet recovered from the effect of Mary's disappearance, and she is in an ill humor with everything and with everybody, which she vents particularly upon her husband, and excuses herself for her want of feeling, by saying that Mary's misfortune had taught her a lesson, and that she will never be a submissive wife, ruled by her husband; and that if her cousin had only taken her advice, instead of being lost to them all, she would now be the acknowledged mistress of Glen Mary.

The evening we make our call we find her distressed indeed, and really grieved, for she has just received a note from Mr. Fairfax, which reads thus:

"*Dear Wife:*—My name as a Fairfax, as well as my honor as a man, requires me to perform a stern duty. I cannot overlook the insult cast upon us, through your relative, by the Grahams, and feel that it can only be wiped out by blood. Therefore I have sent a challenge to Dr. George Graham. It has been accepted, and we meet this evening at four. Before this reaches you, the issue between us will be decided.

"Enclosed, you will find all my instructions as regards the servants and the estate, which I wish carried out to the letter.

"In conclusion, I must say that there is one thought which consoles me in this crisis of my life, and that is that my beautiful young wife will not be grieved, for I have long since known that she never loved me.

"Your husband,
"ALFRED FAIRFAX.
"*September 1st, 18——.*"

Poor Estelle! poor beauty! Poor vain worldling, of what avail to you now is that you have spent years adoring? You are, indeed, at this moment, an object to excite the tenderest sympathy, although Dunreath Abbey, with all its wealth, is yours, and you the recognized queen of society, and sought by all its worshippers. Poor, miserable woman, all that is forgotten now, as, in the agony of suspense and dread, you discover, away down in your heart,— which was almost swallowed up by worldliness— that you do love your handsome, gifted, kind, affectionate husband. You never thought of it before, but you know it now, and you also know that without him this world, with all that it has laid at your feet, would be nothing. Worse, yes, far worse than that, for, as ignorant as you are of Christianity, you know and feel that if he was to return to you safe and unharmed, he would no longer be the noble man that, in your pride, you loved to look upon, but a *murderer*—for what does even the civil law call duelling but wilful, premeditated murder?

Poor wretched girl, even to you, that cannot fully comprehend the awfulness of the crime, for you have never thought of the immensity of the guilt of even the smallest sin against the God of Holiness, and do not know that the wilful murderer calls upon his head the vengeance of heaven. The idea of the husband, of whom you are so proud, being a murderer is fearful, and although you do not pray, we will pray for you, that you will be spared that great grief.

We must leave her now to ascertain the result of the duel, which, we have had an intimation, was to be fought between two "men of honor."

Instead of "Liberty, what crimes are committed in thy name," we might well drop the word "liberty" and substitute "honor," for, of all the senseless, criminal, diabolical customs that rule a corrupt world, the custom young men have of displaying, in a duel, their conceit and vanity before wretches like themselves, is the greatest. The poor fools imagine themselves brave and honorable, when truly they are displaying only love of self, and moral cowardice. If it were not for the criminality of it, it would almost call a smile to our lips when we hear or read of poor idiots wiping out insults by each other's blood. But when we know of Christians conforming to this institution of the devil, men who call themselves followers of their crucified Redeemer, who was led, like a lamb, to the slaughter, and who plainly tells them "You shall not kill," no wonder our lips pale and hearts quail, when we remember that God is infinite in justice, as well as in mercy.

Two of these honorable men are on the field, the ground is measured, their places assigned; the seconds have loaded the pistols and are handing them to the combatants, when, to the surprise of all, Dr. George refuses the weapon, saying:

"No, Alfred Fairfax, I will not fight the man who raises his arm in defence of my injured wife. And if my heart's blood will remove or palliate my offence against her, I want you and the world to know that I willingly, nay, gladly, give it."

Here he exposed his breast to the deadly weapon of his opponent, which was instantly fired into the air, Alfred expressing himself satisfied.

Dr. Graham left the field with a disappointed look upon his face, as if he thought he had been prevented making a martyr of himself.

Oh! man, man! imagining yourself unworthy to remain with frail, sinful man like yourself, and yet willing to go into the presence of Almighty God!

CHAPTER XIV.

WITH our reader's permission, we will pass over an era of two years, and review respectively the characters that figure conspicuously in this life history.

"Honor to whom honor is due." And fulfilling this time-honored maxim, we will commence with Col. Graham who, according to this world's estimate, ranks first in superior worth. We find him much altered from the individual we parted with two short years ago. He is a much older and, we think, a much wiser man; for having committed one mistake, viz.: his cruelty towards his daughter-in-law, he has begun to suspect his infallibility in worldly matters, and we no longer see the dictatorial, bombastic, egotistical Col. Graham of yore; but in his place, a mild old man, who gently expresses opinions, hesitatingly gives advice, and who is affable and kind to all whom he meets. We admire him vastly more than we did, but in this we differ greatly from the world, which has begun to pity the Colonel and think he is fast approaching his dotage.

At the time we are reviewing him, he is engaged in earnest conversation with Dr. Fitzpatrick—for he has begun to think of the one thing necessary. A short synopsis of the conversation we will give.

"Doctor, I can agree with you, that if Christ established a church that was to teach all truth, the

Catholic Church, being the oldest of all Christian churches by fifteen hundred years, must be the one; and this I would as firmly believe as you do yourself, sir, if I did not see that it errs in its practices and its teachings."

"Now, Colonel," replied the Doctor, "let us enquire into some of these erroneous teachings, and let us see if, by a careful and impartial examination, we will not, in the end, surprise ourselves by believing the Church of God to be in the right, and we to be in the wrong?"

"No, Dr. Fitzpatrick, that I can never do, for whilst I'll acknowledge that your Church teaches Christ to be God, and consequently deserves the name of Christian, still it makes gods of others not mentioned in the Godhead. Don't look so surprised, sir, for last year, whilst travelling with my unhappy son through Europe, in the vain hope of reanimating and reviving him by change of scene, I noticed, particularly, that the Catholics were heretical in practice, and was often myself an eye-witnesss to it."

"Name some of those heretical practices, sir?" interrupted the Doctor.

"Well, do not be offended at my remarks, and I will tell you some of the things that I saw," replied the old man. "I saw magnificent edifices of marble and granite, beautiful with walls of agate and jasper, filled with jeweled ornaments and offerings of wealth, and heard them called God's churches; and when I was edified and filled with respect for my fellow-man who would thus deprive himself of what he most loved—gold—to show his love to his Creator, like the woman the Gospel tells us of, who carried the precious ointment in the alabaster box to pour on the feet of our Lord, and entered any of these edifices to adore Christ also, I saw that it was not Him, but His creatures, and especially His Mother, that was worshipped, for I saw the congregation kneeling before Madonnas, worshipping before shrines, and kissing altars of Mary, and all these I protest are heretical practices."

Here the Colonel paused and looked at Dr. Fitzpatrick as much as to say, what I have argued is unanswerable.

The Doctor, interpreting the look, smiled goodhumoredly and answered:

"In reading your Bible, Col. Graham, which, I understand, you have begun to do lately, and which, by the way, is a very good practice, and one we Catholics are fond of indulging in, although the Protestant world protests to the contrary, did you ever think of accusing Abraham, Jacob, Saul, David, and many others I could name, of idolotry?"

"No, certainly not, Dr. Fitzpatrick, and I am at a loss to understand you," replied the Colonel in surprise.

"Why, did you not read of them prostrating themselves to the ground and adoring, respectively, people and angels?"

"I did, sir, but their adoration consisted in the deep veneration they were showing the servants of God, not——"

"The very words you have used," interposed the Doctor, "express the worship paid by Catholics before the altar of the Blessed Virgin. We are not senseless enough to try to make God's creature equal to Himself, nor do we ascribe to her any power, grace, or beauty that was not given to her by her Creator—God."

"I will not say that you do, sir, educated and sensible like you are; but does not your Church, in allowing these practices, even amongst the learned like yourself, draw the ignorant into idolatrous worship?"

"You may, Col. Graham, with as much justice, accuse Protestant parents of making their children idolators, when they allow them to kneel to them for their blessing. No, we are not idolaters, for, in saluting the Mother of God as holy and full of grace, we do no more than the Gospel of St. Luke does; when we call her blessed, we are but fulfilling the prophecy of Scripture—'From henceforth all generations shall call me blessed;' in asking her prayers, if we injure the mediatorship of Jesus, we do the same that St. Paul did when he recommended himself to the prayers of the faithful; and remember it is St. Paul himself who says: 'One is our mediator, Jesus Christ,' and he certainly did not destroy what he taught, or contradict himself, when he begged the prayers of others, like we Catholics do."

"Well, as I said before, Doctor, your argument holds good as regards yourself and others as enlightened as you are, but do not your devotional books, prayer books, catechisms, &c., teach a different doctrine from yours, and are not the unlearned, by such teachings, led into idolatry?"

"Col. Graham, I have many Catholic books at my command, and can get hundreds more, if necessary, of prayer books and catechisms; and if, sir, in one of these books approved by the Church, you can find one single expression that would lead the weakest mind amongst us to do more than beg the Mother of God, the saints, and angels to pray for us, or ascribe to them a power equal to God, or independent of Him, then I will acknowledge myself a member of a Church that errs in its teachings; and furthermore, Colonel, I ask you to ride with me to-morrow to see my patients, for I have amongst them the poorest of the poor, and ignorant enough to convince even you of the poverty of their understanding, and if, among these illiterate people that call themselves Catholics, you can find one who misinterprets the teachings of the Church into idolatry, I will again acknowledge myself mistaken."

"Why, Dr. Fitzpatrick, can you be in earnest about my seeking information in the two ways you have pointed out? If you are, it will not be two hours after I have commenced, until I confound you."

"In earnest about you examining into what we teach? Oh! Colonel, if I could only tell you how anxious we Catholics are for the Protestant world to understand us aright, and how we invite inquiry and pray for it, oh! so earnestly, you would never again doubt my sincerity."

Here we will leave the two gentlemen, and will not join them again until we go with them amongst the impoverished and unenlightened Catholic element in our country, to see if they are heathenish in their practices and worship.

Mrs. Col. Graham and her sister-in-law come next on our list of revision. We find them but little changed. Mrs. Graham is still the dupe of her artful sister, and a nature, naturally sweet, gentle, and loving, is fast becoming embittered and hardened.

Sister Sallie's eyes are brighter, if possible, than ever, her step lighter, and her smile more winning than when last we saw her; the world seems to be treating her kindly and, judging from the brightness of her countenance, we would think that she was succeeding to her heart's desire with all her plans.

Dr. George Graham is a restless wanderer in foreign lands, pausing only long enough, in his hasty flight from place to place, to write a line to his mother to ask: "Have you heard anything of her?" We find him quite another person from the gay young man that was first introduced to our readers. There is now an inexpressible sadness about him, a hungry longing in his eye that insensibly wins upon our compassion, and in spite of our knowledge of his unkindness and rudeness to the fair, gentle girl he had vowed to love and cherish, we can but pity and wish it were otherwise with him.

What is it about Estelle that also calls for our sympathy? Everything seems unchanged with her. The world smiles as sweetly upon the proud, spoiled beauty as of yore, there are as many fawners at her feet feeding her vanity—of which, unhappily, she has a large share—as when last we saw her; but still she is changed, undoubtedly changed, for if we notice her closely we will see an anxious look in her handsome, brown eyes, which is carefully concealed from the casual observer, and a nervous twitching about the corners of her lips—which are now smiling so sweetly—that denotes inward pain. What is it, Estelle? You were not wont to give those nervous starts, and why bend forward so eagerly every time you hear a footfall on the stairs?

There is a step approaching now, a fast, unsteady step that causes the blood to rush in a wild, mad leap to the neck, cheek, and brow of the listening woman. And, as the door is thrown rudely open and Alfred Fairfax staggers, rather than walks, into the room, we are answered.

Estelle, you have done your work well! Blame not rum; it was you that brought him to this; reduced the man in whom was centered all your pride and ambition to the degradation of the brute creation! It is well for you to weep, though tears of blood will not avail you now.

Our little friend Coralie is almost grown; being sweet sixteen, she bids fair to rival Mrs. Caroline in beauty, and her bright, winsome ways make her interesting and attractive to an unusual extent in one so young. Her mother is unchanged and unchangeable, not even a tornado, sweeping everything in its path, and breathing death and destruction, springing up near her, could, even for an instant, make her forgetful of the dignity that she —Mrs. Graham—should preserve. It was only when danger threatened her child that she was at all natural or lost any of her studied art.

We must not close our review without mentioning Viola, to whom we are inclined to be very partial. Compared with Mrs. Col. Graham, on whom was lavished so much unnecessary compassion, we can but feel the unkindness of the world's estimate of human nature. Where Mrs. Graham was weak and uncertain, Viola was strong and reliable; and where the one had no thought but for the few she loved, the other was full of the tenderest sympathy for all the poor wayfarers the globe contains. Yet the injustice of man made an idol of Mrs. Col. Graham, and left Viola friendless and alone. We will not be so unjust, and will recognize the noble character possessed by the neglected girl—warmhearted, generous to a fault, kind and affable, was our favorite.

In the last year a great happiness had been given her. Remembering the advice of Dr. Fitzpatrick, "to seek and find," she sought earnestly the truth and soon found it in the One, Holy, Catholic, and Apostolic Church of God, which the Holy Ghost teaches, and Christ is with to the end of time.

And what matters to her now, whether the world frowns or smiles, if she is or is not friendless. Can she not make friends among the departed servants of God, for she believes in the "Communion of Saints," and that the ones reigning with Christ pray for those that still have to combat the world, the flesh, and the devil. How much consolation she finds in this doctrine, for she can now "hold converse with the venerable prophets and patriarchs of ancient times, with the heroes of Christianity, the blessed Apostles and martyrs, and with the angelic choirs that minister around God's throne."

She is travelling with her invalid mother to some of the many summer resorts in Virginia that are the most renowned for the efficacy of their waters, in the hope of giving strength to the poor sufferer.

CHAPTER XV.

THERE was not a cloud to be seen in the sky, not the motion of a breeze stirred the stillness of the leaves, not even the rippling of the waters, as they went on forever, could be heard. No bird waked its wonted praise to its Maker. All nature seemed determined not to disturb the siesta of Dunreath Abbey's lovely mistress who, on this warm July afternoon, was sweetly resting in utter oblivion of all things. Ever and anon a bright smile would pass over the delicate features of the sleeper's face, and, at times, she seemed scarcely to breathe, so deep was her slumber.

Sitting near, and gently fanning her was rather a queer little old woman dressed in black, with nothing to relieve its sombreness but a small cap, whiter, if possible, than the locks of driven snow it pretended to conceal. Her eyes were covered by green glasses. Resting on either side of her chair was a crutch, that spoke for themselves and told the sad story, that their owner was a cripple. But in spite of them there was something about her that attracted, rather than repulsed you.

Perhaps it was the air of gentle patience, which great trouble nobly borne gives, that won upon you. Certain it was that you would not have passed her by with only a casual glance, but would have paused for an instant before her, if for nothing else but to account to yourself for so doing.

Whilst we are describing her, Estelle opens her wondrous eyes and looks around. As they rest upon the cripple they brighten into recognition.

"Have I been asleep long, Annette?"

"You have slumbered over an hour, lady; but it is quite early yet. Try to rest longer."

"Oh! I would gladly do so if they would only come back."

"Who?" asked Annette in surprise.

"Why, the beautiful creatures of my sleep. I have just awakened from such a beautiful, beautiful dream, which, like Byron's, I think was not all a dream," answered Estelle, as she passed her small hands over her face. "Listen, Annette, whilst I tell it to you.

"I thought I was once more in my childhood's happy home calling mother, to whom I was eagerly wishing to show something I was holding in my hands. Though I searched in every room, she was nowhere to be seen.

"'Mother, mother! where are you?' I cried.

"'Here,' at length answered a voice I knew to be hers, and I saw, far in front of me, the form of my mother, seemingly standing on air, and encircled by a bright, bright light, though its brilliancy did not dazzle the eye, but rather increased the enjoyment of the senses. Her eyes were beaming upon me with a depth of love that seemed to soothe and quiet me.

"'Come to me,' I again implored as I stretched out my arms towards her.

"'It is not permitted, my child,' she gently answered. 'It is you that must come to me.'

"As I started to go, I saw to my surprise that, instead of only a room separating us, it was a wide, wide field, full of briars, rude shrubs, and black, murky streams, with here and there a fierce monster's mouth open to devour, or a serpent coiled to strike.

"'Oh! mother,' I cried as I drew back shuddering, 'I cannot, I dare not!'

"At my refusal and fright, such a look of sorrow and commiseration stole into her face, that I asked:

"'Is there no other way that I can reach you, for I long to be with you and rest.'

"As I spoke she pointed towards you, who, for the first time, I noticed was with me, and her face lighted up with an expression of deep thankfulness as she joyfully said : 'Lean upon her; she will bring you safely through the thicket.'

"In obedience to a sign from her you approached me, and lightly bore me over the briary road, safely by the yawning mouths of the savage beasts, crossed over the huge reptiles, walked on the angry waters until you safely laid me at my parent's feet.

"'Here let me rest always,' I prayed; 'keep me ever near you, my precious mother.'

"'Not yet, my child, not yet; there is work for you to do in the vineyard of the Lord,' she answered; 'but what is it you wish to show me?'

"'Oh! these two bright, glorious jewels, whose lustre, though dim in places, shines with more brilliancy than the stars! Tell me how I can remove the dark spots upon them, and restore them to their owner, dear mother.'

"She bowed her head for a few moments as if in prayer, and then said:

"'The great privilege of beholding the place where they belong is accorded you, Estelle; come with me.'

"We seemed now to be borne by some invisible agency into a country that abounded in fragrant flowers of most delicate hues and tints, musical streams of clearest waters, whose gentle flow was more melodious than the sweetest voice ever waked in song, and numerous birds of rarest plumage and brightest colors. Like ourselves, I noticed travellers seeking this favored country, whose countenances beamed with holiest thanksgivings; the very air of this strange land seemed to speak of peace and joy, and nowhere and in no face were to be seen traces of care or decay.

"Suddenly the birds ceased their songs, the waters their flow, and our hearts stood still as we felt the presence of that blest country's Queen. As she advanced she smiled upon her waiting subjects, and took from the hand of each a jewel resembling those that I was holding; as she touched it, it would lose its spots and become dazzling in its lustre, she would then place it in a crown she held. I was the last she approached; as she came towards me she pointed to the crown of jewels, and I saw that it required but two more to make it complete.

"'Have you got them for me, daughter?' she asked, in a voice of unutterable sweetness.

"'Yes, great Queen,' I answered, 'but they are so tarnished, they are not worthy of the place you have kept for them.'

"'Let me see,' she asked, and as she took them I saw that each jewel was an immortal soul, and the ones I offered were Alfred's and my own.

"'Yes, child,' the gracious Queen said, 'these are the souls I collect each day and offer at my dear Son's feet. You see the place reserved for yours and the other one that you must bring me; all will be dear to our great King.'

"Then I awoke, Annette; but was it not a strange dream? My darling mother! I think I see her yet, and I can never forget the beauty of that glorious Queen."

Annette assented, and for some time neither spoke; then Estelle asked:

"Have you ever had a sorrow? I mean," she added, remembering the crutches, "a sorrow brought on by yourself, the weight of which seemed too heavy to be borne?"

As she spoke she saw the little woman wince, though she answered bravely:

"I have, ma'am, of course known trouble, and who is it that has not? But Heaven holds a balm for every grief if we do but seek it there."

"Yes, yes; so you always tell me. But come, it will be full two hours before Mr. Fairfax can return from B——, that is," she continued with quivering lips, "if he comes at all to-night, and I will listen until then to some more of those beautiful anecdotes and legends of saints, which you can tell so pleasantly, and which are beginning already to make me love your religion."

In a voice full of pathos Annette complied with the request and told story after story of patient suffering, long endured with heroic fortitude, borne by those faithful servants who were once sojourners like ourselves and surrounded with all the trials, distractions, and drawbacks that mar our lives, and who, for those blessings which are so great "that ear hath not heard, eye hath not seen, nor hath it entered the heart of man" the extent of them, silently suffered. Particularly did she dwell on the sweet life of St. Monica, and how for thirty long years she followed her son Augustine, to bring him to repentance.

"Did she at last reclaim him?" interrupted Estelle.

"Yes, after so long a time her perseverance was rewarded by his conversion, which caused him to break out into that beautiful rhapsody to his Creator: 'O Beauty, ever ancient and ever new! Too late have I known Thee, too late have I loved Thee!' Thus was his mother's prayers answered, and the prediction of St. Ambrose, 'that this child of so many tears could not be lost,' verified."

Whilst she is thus trying to pour oil upon the wound that is torturing her listener, let us answer the question that we imagine our reader is impatient to ask, viz.: Who and what is this Annette, and how does it happen that she is Estelle's bosom companion.

About a year before she is introduced, Mrs. Fairfax, who had nothing at all to do, fancying she would like to employ a portion of her time in acquiring a knowledge of the French language, advertised for a competent teacher. From the many applicants for the situation her choice fell upon Annette, though she could not, except from a feeling of pity when she first noticed the crutches in her little hands, account satisfactorily to herself for so doing.

Shortly after her installment as teacher, Estelle discovered that the feeble cripple was necessary to her in a thousand ways. Whenever she needed advice Annette was the only one that could, without saying either too much or too little, acquaint her exactly with what she should do; if in distress of mind or body, who like the little teacher could charm away pain and calm and soothe her agitated feelings.

Her ascendancy over the servants was also wonderful. Loud words or angry disputes would cease directly she approached, and the younger ones used to wonder if she could not use her crutches as wings, and fly like the beautiful angels she used to tell them of. There was but one at the Abbey that avoided the little woman, and that was its master. Evidently, to him her gentle presence was a restraint.

The two hours that Estelle thought it would take for Alfred to make his appearance had come and gone; hour had succeeded hour and still he came not. Midnight was just approaching. Estelle now insisted upon Annette retiring. Though repeatedly urged to do so, she would not leave her mistress to watch and wait alone.

At last the quiet around was broken by loud laughter, rude jests, and dreadful oaths, as a party of revelers neared the house. Loudest and rudest of all rose the voice of Alfred Fairfax, and as it fell on the shuddering ears of the waiting wife, an ashen hue overspread her face, her breath came quickly, and her form swayed to and fro like a tender plant swept by a rude blast.

With clasped hands and streaming eyes she now commanded Annette to leave her. The Frenchwoman, respecting the feeling that made her shrink from exposing her husband's disgrace, arose without a remonstrance, and left the apartment; but not without casting a look of deepest commiseration and tenderest love upon the stricken lady, which told her more than words could say of sympathy.

As her soft step died away in the distance, another was heard approaching fast and unsteady, and shortly afterwards Mr. Fairfax tottered into the room.

"So, so, my beauty! you are sitting up for me, are you? Glad to see your husband back? Aha! Well, why don't you give me a kiss of welcome?" and the drunken brute staggered up to the shrinking woman. "Why, what's the matter? Crying are you? Come, hush up that foolishness; be jolly; with your sniffling and snuffling all the time, you are no company for a man at all. Why, there are two of you! And who are all those men climbing over the walls? See, there are a dozen of them peeping over the door at us! Ha, ha! my lovely, this is the way you spend your time while

I'm away on business, is it? And this is the way I punish you!"

He raised his hand to deal a heavy blow; but fortunately for the poor wife he aimed at the imaginary Estelle, and in so doing fell heavily upon the floor.

"Oh! that men should put an enemy into their mouths to steal away their brains! That we should, with joy, gayety, revel and applause, transform ourselves into beasts."

It is a fearful sight to look upon God's noblest work when he has forfeited his greatest attribute—reason. We have thought that the demons below can scarce be more repulsively frightful than man, crazed and maddened by drink.

How horrible to the young wife was the sight of her husband prostrate by her side. When she saw that he was now unconscious, either from the force of the fall or from intoxication, her anguish was terrible; and worse than all, she could not still the small voice within her breast that kept crying aloud:

"Woman, behold thy work."

Truly remorse is the worst form of anguish. Vainly she called upon him to look at her, or to speak, but all sense had flown. At last, from force of habit, she sought Annette.

Months afterwards she remembered that when, in her haste, she entered the cripple's room without announcing herself, that the little Frenchwoman seemed confused and frightened, and took an unnecessarily long time to relight the lamp that was extinguished as she opened the door, and a strange feeling of the past came over her which, in her trouble and excitement, she did not investigate.

"Can you come and sit with me a while?" she asked. "Mr. Fairfax seems fearfully ill."

"Certainly, ma'am," was the gentle answer. "It is a pleasure to be with you at any time."

When Estelle returned to her room, she found her husband in a sitting position, with his hands held out clasping the air, his head thrown back, and his eyes rolling fiercely from side to side, as he imagined he was driving over difficult and dangerous roads. Every now and then he would curse his imaginary team, and make his listeners tremble.

"What must I do, Annette? For God's sweet sake direct me," implored Estelle.

"Why, send for your physician at once," was the prompt answer.

"Oh! will not this paroxysm pass off?" she replied, with a look that said she was not willing to expose him.

"I fear not," said the cripple; "he is very ill."

"You don't mean to say he has *mania à potu?*" the wife exclaimed with lips of ashen pallor.

"I know not, but it is clearly your duty to send for medical assistance at once."

Estelle made no further objections; her despair and remorse were too deep for words. She thought no more of disgrace; she only realized that her beloved was in danger, perhaps dying. Those happy, happy months that followed her marriage, when her Alfred was all her own, her handsome, kingly Alfred. How bitterly she thought of them.

Oh! if she could but have him that way once more, then how devoted, how tender, how patient she would be. He would never leave her for drink again, never, never.

Often and often, during that long, long morning before light was sent to cheer and gladden the world, did she breathe such vows unto the Lord, who, as Annette had assured her, bent a listening ear to each petition for mercy, invoked by his poor, afflicted children.

Before morning dawned it required the strength of three men, besides Dr. Fitzpatrick, to keep the maniac in restraint, but towards noon he succumbed to the strong nervines administered, and sank into a heavy sleep; and then, as Dr. Fitzpatrick arose to depart, he told Estelle that she might hope that all would soon be well.

"Oh! you must not, must not leave me!" she answered, as she caught his hand convulsively.

"I am compelled to go now, my child, as I have another patient that I must see this evening, but I will return and spend to-night here."

As he shook hands he asked:

"Who is this you have with you?"

"Annette Berdeau is her name," she hesitatingly answered.

"Well, is that all you know of her?" he asked.

"That is all, except that she is the sweetest and the best creature that I ever saw."

"Humph!" grunted the physician as he walked away.

CHAPTER XVI.

"DR. FITZPATRICK, you remember Viola Williams that was visiting us a year or so ago; her mother has been an invalid for a long time, and I have persuaded her to leave the springs and come here for a couple of months, and put herself under your treatment, believing that you can do more towards hastening her cure than all the invigorating waters in Virginia," said Col. Graham, one morning, as the family were seated on the piazza awaiting Mrs. Williams' arrival. On Sallie's brow a dark cloud rested, as she also asked:

"Do you remember her, Doctor?"

"Oh! yes, madam, I remember Miss Viola perfectly well, and will be glad to meet her again."

"I never saw such exuberance of spirits in any one else," the Colonel remarked.

"Poor Mrs. Williams," sighed the sister, "when I think of her so uncomplaining, and so patient, with that heedless, and I am obliged to add, heartless, daughter of hers, I can scarcely keep my tears back."

"Oh! but, Sister Sallie," interrupted Mrs. Graham, a little hesitatingly, as if she was afraid even to venture a remark in the august presence of her sister, "Viola has been nursing her mother for a long time now, depriving herself of every pleasure, and that proves she must have heart."

"I would be happy to think, Susan, that you were not mistaken in regard to her depriving herself of every pleasure for her poor mother's sake; but Caroline wrote me a short time ago that she was taking Mrs. Williams, nolens volens, to the springs, because the Roger family were going."

"And why does she follow that particular family? Are they relations of hers?" queried Dr. Fitzpatrick.

"Not yet," answered Sallie, giving her words a peculiarly significant emphasis, "but—" here she paused for a moment, and then added, with an arch smile, "I don't know that I ought to tell secrets."

"I can infer what you mean," he replied, and to a person far less observant than Mrs. Sallie Graham, it would have been apparent that the Doctor was ill at ease, and no longer watched impatiently for the arrival of the guests. Seeing the effects her words had produced, the cloud cleared rapidly from her brow, and when the carriage bearing the travelers drew near, she was the first to advance to meet them. Viola sprang lightly from the vehicle, and very cordially extended her hand to Sallie, saying:

"Oh! Mrs. Graham, I am so glad to come once more to the Glen, I hope that it will be of benefit to mother."

"It will, I am sure," Sallie replied, as she turned from Viola to Mrs. Williams, and surprised that lady with an affectionate hug, and the shedding of a tear or two as she said, "Welcome to Glen Mary, my dear Madam. Do you feel much fatigue after your long ride?"

"No, not as much as I feared I would," Mrs. Williams answered; "but Viola would not allow the driver to go out of a walk."

Here a violent fit of coughing seized the invalid, which caused her daughter to spring quickly to her side, and draw her head gently down upon her shoulders for support. Just then Dr. Fitzpatrick came up and wished, as he stopped to admire the fair young girl with her arms tenderly and gracefully wound round the aged woman wearily reclining upon her breast, a look of loving commiseration in her dark brown eye, for the talent of an Angelo or a Raphael, to indellibly stamp upon canvass the beautiful, touching picture of youth supporting age. It is said there is some sort of subtle attraction or magnetic influence in a steady gaze that invariably causes the person looked at to become conscious of it, even before the fact is made known to the eye; thus it was with Viola, and it was with burning cheek and throbbing heart that she raised her eyes to encounter the admiration expressed in the physician's glance. He smiled, advanced, and cordially welcomed her back; a sad expression stole over his face, as he looked at Mrs. Williams, and noticed her difficulty of breathing, her bright eyes and the hectic flush on her poor, thin cheeks.

Sister Sallie, apparently with the greatest tenderness and depth of feeling, supporting the invalid on her arm, assisted her into the house, whilst Viola delayed at the carriage to collect the wraps and medicines she had brought for her mother's use on the journey. When Mrs. Williams was out of hearing, she turned to the Doctor, exclaiming: "Oh! Dr. Fitzpatrick, I have brought my mother for you to cure; you will not let her die; tell me what you think of her?"

"I have made no examination yet, Miss Viola, but all that medicine can do to save her shall be done, but you know we physicians are only instruments in the hands of God, and it is only those He wills to live that we cure."

As he spoke thus doubtingly of her mother's safety, he saw the color forsake the face of the fair girl he was looking upon and her small hand tremble, and he smiled to think how mistaken Mrs. Sallie was in supposing she had no heart.

Viola caught the smile, and, imagining it caused by the betrayal of her emotion, said, drawing herself up with something of her old spirit:

"A mother sick unto death is no laughing matter, Dr. Fitzpatrick, and I am at a loss to know the cause of your amusement."

Here the glance of defiance she gave him made the smile return to the Doctor's face which her speech had driven away, as he answered:

"God forbid, Miss Williams, that the distress of one of His creatures should ever be the source of amusement to me."

He was here interrupted by the approach of Col. Graham, who called out "Welcome, welcome, Viola! Child, when you went away you carried with you all our life, and light, so you may judge how glad we are to have you back once more. But what's the matter, Viola?" he added, as he saw the girl's pale face.

"Mother!" was all her trembling lips could say in answer, whilst her eyes filled with tears.

"Oh! cheer up, cheer up, Viola; whilst there is life there is hope, and have we not Æsculapius himself here?" nodding towards the Doctor.

"And what is still better than Æsculapius, Miss Viola," said Dr. Fitzpatrick, "we have the pure mountain air of the heavens, and it will do much, I have no doubt, towards restoring your mother; so you must not despair."

By this time they had reached the house, and Viola was shown to the invalid's room, where she found both the Mrs. Grahams attending kindly to all her mother's wants. After remaining with her guests for some time, and succeeding at last in persuading the sufferer to take a nap before dinner, and upon the others retiring into Sallie's room, so that the invalid would be perfectly quiet, Mrs. Graham withdrew to superintend her house-keeping matters, taking with her Viola and Sallie. After Mrs. Graham left them, the other lady surprised Viola no little by throwing her arms affectionately around her and saying in a faltering voice:

"Darling, I want you to grant me a great favor; there is something in your poor sick mother, that forcibly reminds me of my precious Henry." Here the lady paused for a moment and buried her face in her hands, whilst sobs shook her delicate frame. In a little while she seemed able to conquer her emotion, and then added:

"Perhaps it is because she is suffering from the same disease, and her hollow cough reminds me of him; now the favor, Viola, is—that you will allow me to take your place whilst you are here, and be your mother's nurse. Your pale face and languid eyes show that you require rest, and you need not fear (her voice became tremulous again) to trust her with me."

"Will my consenting to your request, Mrs. Graham," said Viola, really touched at her seeming distress, "banish me from my mother's room?—if it does, I cannot give it."

"Why, child, of course not; you can be there most of your time, but you will allow me the sad comfort of ministering to her wants, and, Viola, she will have a careful, tender nurse; for every breath she draws and every cough that issues from her poor throat, brings back vividly the remembrance of my lost love, and ministering to her would be the greatest consolation."

Viola, somewhat bewildered at Aunt Sallie's manifestation of feeling, hesitatingly gave the required promise, which made her quickly brush away her tears, and after one or two silent embraces of gratitude, she glided lightly to the invalid's room to constitute herself sole nurse. She found Mrs. Williams in a restless slumber from which she soon roused herself, asking for her daughter.

"I am here in Viola's place, while she is resting; let me attend to your wants, my dear madam."

"My head is aching terribly," said Mrs. Williams.

"Then inhale this," the nurse answered kindly,

handing her a phial of aromatic vinegar, whilst at the same time she softly passed her pretty hand across the sufferer's brow. Just at that instant the steps that had been approaching reached the door, and Mrs. Graham ushered in Dr. Fitzpatrick to make an examination of his new patient, and the depth of feeling expressed by Sallie's movements was not lost upon his quick eye.

"Had you not better call Viola?" asked Mrs. Williams, as the Doctor prepared to make his examination.

"She has made me your nurse in her place, my dear madam," pityingly replied the sister, which caused the Doctor to give a start of surprise, Mrs. Graham a significant look, and the invalid to murmur, "The thoughtless, thoughtless child!"

The examination was soon over, and it was with a serious face that Dr. Fitzpatrick left the Glen, for he knew that another immortal soul would soon be called to render up its final account before a just as well as a merciful God.

When Viola was left alone she fell on her knees, and prayed long and earnestly for the strength to say, "Thy will be done," if it was the Divine Will for her beloved parent to be taken away from her. When her prayer was over, she sought the sick woman's chamber, and in that affectionate tone of voice which only a daughter's heart can produce, asked her if she did not feel better.

"I think I do," was the reply, "for I have a good nurse," smiling towards the younger Mrs. Graham, "who knows how to charm away pain."

Viola gave her a look full of gratitude, and gently took her place by her mother's side, which she was allowed to keep until it was time for the physician's arrival the next day. As the hour appointed for his coming drew near, Sallie said:

"You look fatigued, Viola, dear; you must go out and breathe some fresh air, and recreate a while."

"Yes, darling," spoke the mother, "I do not need you now, take your hat and go walking, child, and remember you are forbidden my presence until the roses are restored to your cheeks."

"But, mother——"

"Do not forget your promise, Viola," interrupted Sallie, handing her her hat.

Viola, sighing, arose, and kissing her mother tenderly and affectionately, she left the room. After reaching the lawn she paused, not knowing in what direction she would walk. Looking around, her eyes fell upon the little summer house where Dr. Fitzpatrick had once consoled her and had pointed out to her the true life she should lead. She went rapidly towards it, entered, and sat down in the place where, two years before, she was seated when that good man told her all that was required of her. As she thought of him, and remembered how kindly he had spoken to her, the roses her parent longed for mantled her cheeks and she no longer appeared the dejected, tired girl of a few moments before.

When the Doctor entered the sick chamber he glanced rapidly around to see if Viola was still remiss in her duty to her dying mother. Young Mrs. Graham interpreted the look and answered it, saying: "Miss Williams is out for recreation, but has left me to fill her place here."

"And does she not think that you need recreation also?" he asked.

"Oh! I never think of self when others need me," was the soft response.

"You do seem truly unselfish," he replied, in a low, tender voice, whilst he gazed admiringly upon the bewitchingly fascinating woman before him.

Mrs. Sallie's heart beat violently, and a shy, modest look, which, for once, was not assumed, came into her face as she heard his words, and felt his look of approval and admiration fixed upon her, which greatly enhanced her rare beauty, and made her appear lovely, indeed. Unfortunately for her a violent fit of coughing followed by a slight hemorrhage from the invalid prevented any further remarks, as it required all the Doctor's skill and attention to give relief to the sufferer.

After he succeeded in subduing the paroxysm, he left the Glen. On the lawn he encountered Viola, who was impatiently awaiting his coming to learn his opinion of her mother's case, and who rapidly advanced to meet him. To her "good-morning, Dr. Fitzpatrick," he merely bowed and passed quickly on, leaving the girl surprised and hurt at his rudeness and wondering how she had been unfortunate enough to give him offense.

CHAPTER XVII.

ONE morning as Col. Graham and Dr. Fitzpatrick were riding over the farm belonging to the Glen, the Colonel reminded him of his promise to take him amongst his patients to make inquiries into their religious belief.

"Well," answered the Doctor smilingly, "we are at Michael Harrington's now, a poor man who was unfortunate enough to become my patient the other day by breaking his leg. You may say to him or ask him anything you please, for the love of his religion fills his true Irish heart, and he naturally likes to talk about what he most loves. You will be astonished, Colonel, to find out what good theologians people of his class and religion are, let them be ever so ignorant upon other subjects."

"And how do you account for it, Dr. Fitzpatrick?"

"Why, our Church is very careful to instruct all of her children in the true faith," the Doctor replied.

Here the two gentlemen dismounted and entered the house by a small passage, which led immediately into the sick man's room.

"Good morning, Michael; how are you this morning?" inquired his physician.

"Oh! I'm getting on pretty well, sir," he replied, "thanks be to God and His blessed Mother!"

"Glad to hear it, Michael. Here is Col. Graham that has come to see you," said the Doctor.

"Welcome, Colonel, and it is good of you, so it is, to come to see a poor sick man like me," answered Harrington, extending his hand to the Colonel.

"No, no, Mr. Harrington, it is only our duty to visit the sick, and I deserve no credit for it. But what is that you hold in your hand?"

"Sure, it's my beads, sir. Well, now didn't you know?" replied Michael as he rocked his head backward and forward on his pillow, expressive of his astonishment.

"I must acknowledge my ignorance," Col. Graham answered, a little amused; and, winking slyly at the Doctor, he added, "you pray to this string of beads, don't you?"

"You mean, sir, I use it as a prayer book. You didn't mean to say that I was foolish enough to pray to beads, did you, sir?" asked Michael in surprise.

"Well, how can you use it as a prayer book?" Col. Graham asked, still amazed.

"Why, here I am, sir," Michael answered, "prostrated with sickness, and my throbbing temples will not let me read at all, at all; and I take up my beads and hold the crucifix, which represents to me the death of our Lord, and I say the Apostles' Creed; then touching the first bead brings to my mind the Lord's Prayer, and when I come to one of these large ones—pointing to the five large beads, one of which occurs between every two decades—I name a mystery in our Lord's life, sir."

"Explain what you mean about the mysteries," interrupted the Colonel, now really interested.

"Well, sir, to-day I say the sorrowful ones," the sick man replied. "On the first one I name our Lord's Agony in the Garden of Gethsemane, and I try to think of all our dear Lord suffered for us, while I say the 'Angelic Salutation' ten times on these smaller ones, ending each salutation with 'Holy Mary, Mother of God, pray for us now and at the hour of our death, amen.' Then I come to the next large bead, sir, and on that I name the 'Scourging at the Pillar,' and then I think of all our Lord suffered for us whilst he was fastened at the pillar and whipped, sir; and then I go on as before till I come to the next one, and on that I name the 'Crowning with Thorns.' The next is the 'Carriage of His Cross,' and the last one of this part of the Rosary, sir, is the 'Crucifixion of our Lord Jesus Christ,' and every time I say it, I love Him more and more who suffered so much for me; and I think my beads make a very good prayer book for the likes of them who don't know how to read, sir."

"Well, I would think so too, Michael," said Col. Graham, "if you did not take away from the Son, by praying to the Mother."

"How is that, sir?" asked Harrington, in amazement.

"Why, don't you make the Mother equal to the Son by praying to both of them?"

"No, no, Colonel, we couldn't do that. We beg the divine Son to have mercy on us; but only ask the blessed Mother to pray for us, just like we would ask you, sir; and speaking of that I hope that you will pray for me, sir, for I feel very bad indeed, Colonel," said the sick man.

"Well, but, Harrington, does not your Church teach you that the Virgin Mary is equal to God?" queried Col. Graham.

"Faith, no, sir, it would be blasphemy, sir, to say that one of God's creatures was equal to Him. Here, this book will tell about it, sir," reaching to a table near him on which were several old books, and selecting one, an abridged copy of "The Papist Represented and Misrepresented," "that Father John left me the last time he was here. Now, if you please, turn to page 78 and see what it says about it, sir."

The Colonel very quickly found the page and, to his astonishment, read as follows:

"Cursed is he that believes the saints in Heaven to be redeemers, that pray to them as such, or gives God's honor to them, or to any creature whatsoever, amen. Cursed is every goddess worshipper that believes the blessed Virgin Mary to be any more than a creature, that worships her, or puts trust in her more than in God, that believes her above her Son, or that she can, in anything, command Him, amen."

"That is what our Church teaches, Col. Graham," Michael said as the Colonel stopped reading.

Here Dr. Fitzpatrick arose, saying:

"I think, Harrington, you had better not talk any more just now; you might cause your fever to rise again. We will go now, Col. Graham, and any further questions you wish answered you can ask some of my other patients."

"I have only one more to ask Mr. Harrington, and then I am done," answered the Colonel.

"Did this Father John give you a Bible to read when he gave you this book the other day?"

"Faith, and that he didn't, sir," answered Michael.

"I thought as much," Col. Graham replied, with a look of triumph towards the Doctor. "He wouldn't give you that to read, my good man, would he?"

"Och, no, sir, it would be no use, for I have already three here by me," the sick man said, pointing to the table before mentioned.

"Try to keep quiet, now, until I come to-morrow, and I will loosen your bandage for you," interrupted Dr. Fitzpatrick.

"Oh! then do, sir, and may the Lord reward you for all your kindness to me," replied Michael, with tears in his eyes, as the gentlemen walked out, gently closing the door after them.

A short ride brought them to the next patient, Ann Sullivan, who had been sick for some time with fever, but was now convalescent and able to walk about, but not strong enough to work.

Upon entering, they found her kneeling before a small image of the blessed Virgin holding tenderly the Infant Jesus in her arms. After the preliminary remarks, the introduction of Col. Graham, and feeling of the pulse was over, the Colonel asked:

"Were you not praying when we came in, Mrs. Sullivan?"

"Yes, sir, I was asking the blessed Mother and the saints to thank our good Lord for making me well again, which I never expected to be, sir."

"But, my good woman, how do you know that the saints and the Virgin hear your prayers to them?"

"Why, sir, the Holy Bible says, that there is joy in Heaven over one sinner that repenteth, and they must know up there, in that blessed Country, what we do and say down here, and read our hearts too, or they would not know when to rejoice, sir; and it tells me too, sir, of golden vials full of odors, which are the prayers of the saints, and that proves that they must pray for us, sir."

"Where ma'am, can you find that in the Bible, about the prayers of the saints. I never remember to have read it?" asked Col. Graham.

"In the book of Revelations, sir, the eighth verse of the fifth chapter, will tell you about it. And then you know, sir, we read in St. Matthew what our dear Lord said about the children, that 'their angels do always behold the face of My Father, who is in Heaven,' and that proves that we have guardian angels to protect and take care of us, sir," replied the woman.

"You seem to have read your Bible very carefully, Mrs. Sullivan. I thought your Church did not allow its members to read it."

"Ah! no, sir, you are mistaken, here is one now,

if you would like to look at it," handing him quite an old-looking book.

"Well," said Col. Graham, "this does seem to have been pretty well read; but don't you know, good woman, that this blessed book tells you that there is but one mediator between God and man—the man Christ Jesus?"

"Oh! yes, sir, there is but one," Mrs. Sullivan answered.

"Then why, my good woman, do you make mediators out of the saints?" inquired the Colonel.

"Faith, sir, I never make mediators of salvation out of any of them, the Lord preserve us! I only ask them to pray for me," exclaimed Ann.

"Why, don't you content yourself praying for yourself. God will hear you, won't He?" the Colonel asked.

"Oh! yes, sir. He tells every poor sinner to come to Him, sir, but that holy book tells us that the Almighty, praise be to His blessed Name, commanded the friends of Job to obtain his prayers for the pardon of their sins, and tells us to pray one for the other, sir; and St. Paul himself begged other folks to pray for him, sir, and talking of that, won't you pray for me sometimes? for a poor sinner like me needs all the prayers she can get, sir," replied Mrs. Sullivan.

"Yes, yes, I will," quickly spoke the Colonel, at the same time trying to avoid the quizzical look the Doctor gave him; "but now tell me, Mrs. Sullivan, why were you praying before an image when I came in; do you believe it can help you any?"

"May the blessed Lord preserve me! No, sir," said Ann, horrified at the question. "Why, one of the first questions in my catechism that Father Walters, the best poor man in the whole country, used to teach me long ago, is: May we pray to relics or images? And the answer says: No, by no means, for they have no life or sense to hear or help us, sir."

"Well, why use them at all?" again avoiding looking at Dr. Fitzpatrick, the Colonel asked. "And don't you know, Mrs. Sullivan," he added, "that one of the Lord's Commandments says: 'that you must not make to yourself any graven thing, or the likeness of anything in the Heavens above, or the earth beneath?'"

"Yes, sir, but it adds: 'to adore and serve them;' for if it meant that we couldn't make them at all, we couldn't have our holy Lord's picture in the Bible, sir, or our own pictures, or any coins of the different ages, sir," Ann answered.

"All that is very true, Mrs. Sullivan, but you can't show me a command in the Bible for making images, whilst I have shown you one for not making them."

"Oh! but I can, then, sir, and one of them was given shortly after our blessed Lord told Moses that he must not make any graven thing. The eighteenth verse of the twenty-fifth chapter of Exodus tells Moses he must make two images out of pure gold; and the eighth verse of the twenty-first chapter of Numbers tells him again to make a brazen serpent and set it up for a sign; and that proves, sir, that when our good God gave the commandment that thou shalt not make any graven thing, or the likeness of anything in the heavens above, or the earth beneath, or the waters under the earth, He meant, as the next verse says, to adore and serve them, sir, for He would not contradict Himself, or make Moses break His commandment a few days after He had given it, sir."

"Well," said the Colonel, feeling himself foiled, and snatching up a crucifix from the table and throwing it on the floor, "if you don't believe it has any life or sense, trample and spit upon it and then I will credit what you say."

Ann's sick, pale face crimsoned at this insult shown to the symbol of her religion. With a trembling hand she reached down, took up the crucifix, and piously pressed it to her lips before she spoke reproachfully as follows:

"Would you trample and spit upon the Bible, sir, if I was bad enough to throw it on the floor?"

"No, I would not," answered Col. Graham, "because the Bible relates to Christ and represents His Word. But why did you kiss the crucifix?"

"For the same reason that you would kiss the Bible, sir," replied Mrs. Sullivan. "For the same reason that you would not trample upon your Bible, I would not spurn the crucifix, sir, because it relates to Christ and represents Him dying upon the cross; and for the very same reason that you keep your father's and mother's pictures to remind you of them, I keep these images to keep my mind from straying whilst I'm praying, sir."

"I'll acknowledge," the Colonel answered, "that I am surprised that you understand it in that way. But now tell me, Mrs. Sullivan, what excuse can you give for keeping relics of the saints, and honoring them?"

"Why, Col. Graham, did you never read in your Bible, that when the dead man was let down and touched the bones of Elisha, he revived and stood upon his feet (2 Kings, xix, 21; Acts, xix, 12), and surely all the sick people that were cured from the handkerchiefs and aprons brought from the body of St. Paul, honored them."

"Well, one more question, and I will not trouble you any further, Mrs. Sullivan. Tell me distinctly what your Church teaches about this image and relic worship?" said the Colonel.

"Why, sir, it teaches: Cursed is he that commits idolatry, that prays to images or relics, or worships them for God, amen" (from the Papist Represented and Misrepresented), Mrs. Sullivan replied.

Here Col. Graham expressed himself satisfied that Catholics were not idolaters, and bidding the sick woman "good morning," the two gentlemen left. They rode in silence for some time, Dr. Fitzpatrick thinking it best for the Colonel to commune with his own thoughts, and inwardly praying that the grace would be vouchsafed him both to know and embrace the truth.

The silence was at last broken by Col. Graham saying:

"The change, from the noise and bustle of the springs, to the quiet of our Glen, together with the pure air of the mountains, seems to have had quite a beneficial effect upon Mrs. Williams. I noticed that, for awhile yesterday, she was able to walk around the grounds, and seemed really interested by the attractions of the place. Do you not consider her decidedly improved?"

Dr. Fitzpatrick sighed, and then slowly answered:

"Of course. No physician, be he ever so perfect in the science of medicine, can tell the exact time the lamp of life will be extinguished; but I very much fear that her light will be quickly consumed, for experience has taught me that it is not unusual, with her disease, for the patient to cease to suffer and gain unnatural strength when the lamp of life is almost gone."

"I am distressed, indeed," replied the Colonel, "that such is your opinion, both on our own account, for we will lose an estimable lady, and on account of her poor daughter."

"As regards the latter, I think it is compassion entirely thrown away, for I am certain that I never saw such an unfeeling child before," impulsively interposed the Doctor.

"Well, one would so suppose," returned Col. Graham; "but you must remember that Sallie has taken the entire charge of Mrs. Williams upon herself, and perhaps Viola does not see the necessity of attending to her poor, sick mother."

"Your sister," said the physician, "seems quite the reverse of Miss Williams. She is all charity and sweetness. I do not think I ever knew a more unselfish character."

"Ah! she is a noble woman," replied Col. Graham enthusiastically. "I wish you could have seen all her patience and gentleness with my poor brother, who was a great sufferer for some time before his death."

Whilst this conversation was going on, Viola was saying to the lady discussed:

"You are so very kind to my mother that I don't know how to thank you. Do you know that, at one time, I nourished unkind thoughts of you, and had set you down for anything or everything but just what you are? I am now heartily ashamed for ever being rude or impertinent to you, or believing you aught but the sweetest, the best, and the dearest creature in the world. How can I ever tell you, or even give you an idea, of how grateful I am?"

"Show your gratitude, dear, by allowing me to continue waiting upon her," Sallie answered.

"Oh! Viola," she went on, "you can't know what a consolation it is to me to be allowed to nurse her. I feel, all the time, as though I was ministering to my lost darling once more."

Here tears stopped her utterance, and the girl, wondering how she could ever have wronged, even in thought, a person so full of kindness, tenderly wound her arms about her, and gently drew her head upon her breast.

A few weeks after this we will find the females of the family again assembled in the sick lady's chamber. Mrs. Col. Graham was speaking to the invalid, whose couch was drawn into one of the bay windows overlooking the principal road that led to the house. In the window opposite, Sallie was conversing in low tones with Viola.

"I tell you that Dr. Fitzpatrick does not think your mother in any immediate danger, and there is no use in your confining yourself so closely to this sick room. You must ride this evening, and try the horse brother gave me yesterday. She is said to be perfectly gentle."

"Oh! as regards her gentleness," answered the girl, "I am a first-rate horsewoman, and rather prefer a spirited animal than otherwise; but, Mrs. Sallie," she continued, "please do not insist upon my leaving mother this afternoon, for something tells me I should not go."

"What are you saying, Viola?" asked the mother, whose quick ear caught her last words.

"I was saying that I did not wish to leave you this evening, mother dear," her daughter answered, advancing towards her.

"And I have been pleading with her to go out, and breathe some fresh air, and bring the color back to her pale face by a short canter on my new horse," spoke the sister.

"Yes," put in Mrs. Graham, "you do look pale and dejected, Viola. A ride, I am sure, would do you good.

"Then go, my child," said Mrs. Williams. "I insist upon it, dear," she continued, as she saw Viola's reluctance to leave.

"Oh! mother, darling, do not ask me to go away from you," Viola pleaded, sinking upon her knees by the couch. "Indeed, indeed, a ride will not give me any pleasure."

"But it will be pleasant to me to know that you are exercising in the open air, and besides, I can see you for some distance from this open window. You must obey me, my child."

Viola said no more. She embraced tenderly her suffering parent, and walked silently to the door. As she opened it, she met Dr. Fitzpatrick coming in; with a slight bow of recognition she passed on into her room, and was soon attired for her ride.

"Look, Mrs. Williams," called out Sister Sallie a few moments afterwards, at the same time gently raising the sick woman's head, "Viola is mounting now."

"Where is she going?" asked the Doctor hurriedly.

"'On pleasure bent,'" Sallie answered significantly.

Dr. Fitzpatrick beckoned her to one side, and whispered excitedly:

"Call her back, call her back; this is no time for pleasuring. Gangrene set in this morning, and she," pointing towards his patient, "has not more than an hour of life."

"Alas! Doctor," the sister-in-law answered in a low, trembling voice, "I have just told that heartless girl your opinion, but it seemed not to have the slightest effect upon her. I think it useless to call her back."

With a heavy sigh, Dr. Fitzpatrick resumed his seat by the sick lady's couch, and did not leave it until the soul of Mrs. Williams winged its way into eternity.

A very short ride convinced Viola that Mrs. Sallie was mistaken as to the gentleness of the steed she rode. She was young, spirited, and scarcely bridle wise. However, she felt herself mistress of the situation, and did not give a thought to the danger she was in. Her heart was too full of her mother, her poor, sick mother, who had seemed so pale and wan all the day, and Viola trembled as she asked herself if that strange look in her parent's eye was an assurance of the return of the health and strength that they all said had been given her.

Here she paused and gave the bridle such a sudden and violent jerk, that the mare reared, and would have fallen backwards upon the rider, had she not released her hold of the rein, and thrown herself upon the horse's neck, which action brought her to her feet again. This effort seemed to satisfy the horse for awhile and she stood motionless, whilst Viola repeated the question to herself, if all had not told her that the beloved sufferer was being restored to health? "Yes, all have said so," she answered herself again and again, each time more fully convinced that she was mistaken.

"It is true," she went on, "that I have not heard Dr. Fitzpatrick say so; but Mrs. Sallie has told me repeatedly that such was his opinion, and she surely could have no object in deceiving me in such a case. And yet—" here a thought suggested itself, which, although she dismissed it at once as an unworthy suspicion, determined her to return at once to her mother's side. But she found this no easy matter, for the animal she was riding showed a determined opposition to returning, and try as she would, she could not get the "gentle creature," as the sister-in-law had designated her, turned towards Glen Mary

At last, after using every effort at persuasion, and finding the bridle and whip also vain, Viola dismounted, and tried to lead the unruly steed in the direction of the Glen, thinking, after proceeding a short distance, she could remount and soon be at home In this, however, she was mistaken, for no sooner did the mare find herself free, than she gave a loud neigh, bowed her head as if bidding adieu, violently shook herself, and departed, leaving Viola alone and discomfited, some miles from home and, what was still worse, from a suffering mother.

For an instant a smile radiated her face, as she saw the horse turn a sharp angle in the road and disappear from sight; but as she remembered her situation, so far away from Glen Mary, she could not banish entirely the awful thought that would come back. She sighed wearily, and, with difficulty, repressed her tears. Gathering up in her hands the heavy folds of her riding skirt, she commenced her homeward walk. A glance at the sun showed her it was late in the afternoon, and the poor girl hurried on, not thinking, that if she was to accomplish her long journey on foot, she must take it gently at first, and gradually increase her speed.

On and on she went, until the last rays of the evening's sun had sunk to rest behind the mountain, and the heavy shades of night were lowering thick and fast upon the earth. Tired and exhausted, she paused, clasped wildly her hands to her face, and prayed fervently, earnestly asking the care and protection of her Heavenly Father in her present difficulties. When she removed her hands from her face, as if in answer to her entreaties, she saw a vehicle approaching, and it was still light enough for her to recognize it as Dr. Fitzpatrick's.

"Oh!" she said with a sigh of relief, "he will take me safely home; but then—" she stopped, as a remembrance of his coldness and indifference, lately, came over her, "perhaps," she continued, sighing, "it would be wrong to ask him," and she shrunk into a corner of the fence to hide as he passed.

"Why, Miss Williams, you here, and on foot, too? What is the matter?"

"My horse got away from me, sir, and I am endeavoring to walk to Glen Mary," she answered.

"Well, judging from your difficulty of breathing, I don't think that you will accomplish it; let me assist you in here. I can take you there in a little while."

"Thank you, sir," said Viola, taking the hand extended to her, and springing lightly into the buggy; "I feel so relieved, for night is approaching so rapidly."

After this nothing was said for awhile, when the girl suddenly asked:

"How did you find my mother this evening?"

The physician winced. As heartless as he believed the girl beside him to be, it was painful to tell her that her mother had breathed her last among strangers, whilst she, her unnatural daughter, was away enjoying herself.

"I found Mrs. Williams very ill," he answered, slowly and emphatically.

"Oh! you do not mean that she is in actual danger?" cried Viola, in a tremulous voice.

"I am sorry to tell you that such was my opinion."

"My mother, my poor mother! how mistaken I have been. Please drive faster, Dr. Fitzpatrick!"

"That will be of no avail; your mother does not need you now," said the Doctor, in a sad, reproachful tone.

"Is mother dead?" Viola asked, in a cold, calm, unnatural voice, which made the man addressed start, for his medical ear knew that such tones issued only from breaking hearts, and that the grief that caused them was the most dangerous of ailments.

"My poor child," he answered kindly, "God knows best, and if he wishes to call one of his children home, we must not complain."

His companion answered not, and for the rest of the ride she sat quietly by his side, with not even the movement of a muscle.

When they reached the Glen, the cold hand which he took in assisting her from the buggy sent an icy thrill through him, and he compassionately accompanied her to the room where remained all that was left of the gentle mother who had guided her infant steps, who had been her confidant in girlhood, and her womanhood's dearest friend.

"My God!" she exclaimed, as she stood beside

the lifeless clay, "forgive my mother her offences against Thee, as I forgive the woman who deprived me of her blessing, and her of the consolation of having her only child with her in her dying hour!" Here the afflicted one could say no more; she sank upon the floor as unconscious as the lifeless form at her side.

CHAPTER XVIII.

ANOTHER year is added to the many for which man will have to give a reckoning to a just as well as a merciful God, and one who calls Himself the "God of vengeance." Oh! could we but remember always that our Father in Heaven is infinite in all His attributes, and that justice is one of them; or could we but form the remotest idea of the enormity of the slightest offence against His majesty and sanctity, we would be more apt to work out our salvation in fear and trembling as commanded. We are wont to console ourselves too much with reflections on His mercy and love for us, thinking that a late repentance and the publican's prayer will be all-sufficient, forgetful that our hearts are laid open to His all-searching eye.

We remember an anecdote we heard once about some little girls, which made a deep impression upon us, and which we think well to insert here.

Three or four children were together, and in childlike language were making resolutions to be good. They were all going to commence the next week. One determined to do always what papa and mamma required of her; another was going to own up always and tell nothing but the truth; a third said she was never going to give her mamma any more trouble about not keeping herself neat and clean, &c.

Of this little group one remained silent and thoughtful, until the others wanted to know what was the matter? what was she thinking of, and what was she going to do?

"I was thinking," she answered, with quivering lips and eyes full of tears, "that we cannot fool God."

If men and women would only think as that little child, how much of self-love would be removed.

"The melancholy days" had returned again, and all nature around Glen Mary spoke of decay, notwithstanding she had enrobed herself in the varied beauties of silver sheen and many colored leaves, when one bright, frosty morning Mrs. Sarah Graham came walking towards the Glen, lightly rustling the leaves that had already fallen, and carrying a market basket upon her arm. The cool, bracing, October air, together with the exercise she had been taking, had brought a bright color to her cheek, which caused her handsome black eyes to sparkle with more than ordinary brilliancy and made her appear even lovelier than ever to the almost enraptured gaze of Dr. Fitzpatrick, who, upon her approach, had hastily descended the steps of the gallery to take the basket and assist the lady into the house.

"Why, where so early this cool morning?" he said, offering his hand to relieve her of the load she carried.

"On charity bent," she answered smiling sweetly, and then went on in a low, modest voice:

"I have been miserable ever since you described to me the destitute condition of the Hudson family, and for the last week or ten days, as early as this every morning, I have carried them a breakfast of fried chicken, light rolls, boiled eggs, &c., and have been more than repaid for my trouble by the pleasure it gave me to witness those poor children literally devour the edibles I carry them. Yes, all of them, except one little boy, seem to think it would be wrong to stop until all was eaten; and that one, Dr. Fitzpatrick, has been sick since the first day I saw the family, and this morning I'm afraid is seriously ill, for he seemed to be in a high fever, and I thought at times as I sat near him that his mind wandered."

"I trust," the man addressed answered in an anxious voice, "that you did not sit between him and the door, and that you were near him only a little while?"

As Sallie perceived the anxious tenderness betrayed in the voice of the questioner, her heart throbbed wildly with delight; but as a thought of the danger she had exposed herself to came over her, she grew pale and trembled as she answered:

"Each morning that I have been there I always sat near him, and have frequently washed and dressed him in some clothes I carried to distribute amongst them. Strange I did not once think, he might be suffering from some contagious disease."

"Let us hope that he is not," the Doctor replied, and his voice expressed deep concern as he lowered it, and caught gently the small, white hand that was lying in close proximity to his own. "But be more careful of yourself in future, Mrs. Graham, both on your own account, and on account of the many to whom you are dear."

Here a call to breakfast prevented any further conversation between the two, much to the lady's annoyance, for she was just congratulating herself inwardly, that the goal for which she had so longed and intrigued was at last in her grasp, and it was provoking that such a little thing as a breakfast bell should oppose an insurmountable barrier to her attaining it at once.

Directly the meal was over, Dr. Fitzpatrick mounted his horse and rode rapidly in the direction of the house occupied by the Hudsons. Not long afterwards Col. Graham received a note from him which said:

"COLONEL GRAHAM.

"*Dear Sir:*—I am very sorry to inform you that the child your sister visited, washed and dressed this morning is now in the last stage of small-pox. I trust Mrs. Graham has been vaccinated recently. Prevent all further communication between your family and the Hudsons, and advise Mrs. Graham to burn at once the clothes she wore this morning. In haste.

"Yours, &c.,
"J. FITZPATRICK."

The intelligence this note conveyed had an almost stunning effect upon the poor Colonel. He called his wife, and when she, too, was made acquainted with its contents, she almost fainted from the fright which it occasioned.

"How can we tell Sallie?" she asked in an imploring voice of her husband, as if she hoped he would answer that it was not necessary at all to acquaint her with her danger.

"Of course we must tell her of the risk she has run, and the danger she has incurred," he said, interpreting the tone of her voice correctly; "and, moreover, we will be obliged to ask her, for your sake, dear wife, and for the sake of Caroline and her daughter, whom you remember arrived last night, to retire to 'Oakland' for a short time, until we are sure that she has not contracted the dreadful disease she was unfortunate enough to come in contact with."

"It is fortunate that Caroline and Coralie have not left their rooms yet, and consequently have not seen Sister Sallie since they came. But who will tell her?" went on the wife, bursting into tears. "I am sure that I cannot."

Just then a young, pale girl entered the apartment softly. Her robes of deep black gave her such a sombre appearance that we would never recognize in the quiet maiden the Viola of a year or two back. As she glanced at the Colonel's troubled face, and saw Mrs. Graham's agitation, she advanced towards them to learn the cause of their distress.

Unable to speak, Col. Graham handed her Dr. Fitzpatrick's note. When she finished reading it, Mrs. Graham spoke:

"Oh! Viola, we can never, never tell her of the horrible danger she is in, and that she will be obliged to leave Glen Mary."

"Allow me the sad privilege of acquainting your sister, and, if she is forced to leave you for a while, the permission of going and staying with her until your minds are relieved of all apprehension."

"What, you, Viola, I thought that you and Sister Sallie were not on the most amicable terms, and here now you are willing to risk your life for her sake," returned Mrs. Graham.

"She is now in trouble," the girl answered gently, and when the required permission was given, she again softly left the room to carry the distressing news to the one most concerned. The horror of "Sister Sallie," when she was compassionately informed of her danger, was greater than language can describe, so we will not dwell on her terror.

Viola burned all the clothes she had worn, and kindly assisted her in making preparations to leave Glen Mary. To go, Sallie was more than willing, for Oakland had always been a delightful and favorite resort of the Grahams, and was not more than ten miles distant, and had an additional attraction far above any other to her, which was its nearness to Avoca, the home of the man she loved.

Her surprise at Viola's willingness to accompany her, and to be her nurse if stricken with the loathsome disease she so much dreaded, was very great, for she knew nothing of the religion which teaches us to love our enemies and to do good to those who hate us; and if she could have felt grateful, she would have done so, as she noticed, when leaving the Glen, Mrs. Caroline and the other inmates of the house fleeing from her as if she were some vile thing that it would defile them to touch.

During the short ride which brought them to their destination, Viola felt unusual compassion for the excited, nervous, and helpless woman at her side, whom she felt powerless to rescue from her danger. After silently praying for her, she addressed her in words of cheer, and begged her to try and compose herself.

"Oh! it is very well for you to talk, Viola Williams, for if you do take the abominable disease I dread so much, you would not have any beauty to lose, but to think of me, of this face, which he thinks so lovely, pock-marked, and so disfigured that he can never gaze with pleasure on it again. Oh! the very thought of it very nearly distracts me."

A slight tremor passed through Viola's frame, as the little word "he" was significantly emphasized, but she quietly mastered herself and answered:

"I remember an anecdote about my favorite poet, Moore, which I think suits your case. His wife, who was very beautiful, was unfortunate enough to contract small-pox, and although she recovered her health, her beauty was forever lost. This caused her much sorrow, for, like you, she dreaded the loss of the love that she prized more than life. It was a long time before Moore could discover the cause of her dejection; when he did so, he instantly wrote that touching little melody, 'Believe me, if all those endearing young charms,' which he presented to her, and which removed all her fears, and restored her happiness."

"I do not remember the poem you speak of," Mrs. Graham answered. "Is it one of the Irish melodies?"

"Yes, and if you will lean your poor head here on my shoulder, I will sing it for you," Viola said, gently drawing the lady's head upon her breast, and commencing the song in a sweet and gently modulated voice.

As the last stanza

"No the heart that has truly loved never forgets,
But as truly loves on to the close,
As the sunflower turns on her god when he sets,
The same look which she turned when he rose."

died softly away, Mrs. Graham asked:

"Viola, do you agree with him, that the heart that has truly loved never forgets?"

"Yes, that I do," she answered enthusiastically, "and know that all the romance, nobleness of soul, and imaginary heroic qualities attached to the first love, can never be given to the second."

"Then you do not think it mere beauty that man loves?"

"Beauty, without virtues to ennoble it, sinks into insignificance," answered Viola, we must acknowledge rather bitterly.

"Oh! then, if I were only worthy of his love," murmured the afflicted woman.

"Strive to be worthy of a love greater than he: 'Seek first the Kingdom of Heaven, and all things will be added unto thee,'" Viola whispered gently into the ear of the sufferer leaning upon her for support.

By this time the carriage had reached Oakland, and both ladies were greatly surprised to see Dr. Fitzpatrick awaiting them, who had been apprized of Mrs. Graham's arrival by the Colonel.

He assisted Sister Sallie very tenderly into the piazza, and a look of deep commiseration stole into his face, as his practiced eye noticed the first symptoms of that fearful disease which is a scourge to all mankind. He turned to the person who had accompanied her, expecting to greet Mrs. Col. Graham, when, to his astonishment, he saw Viola.

"You here!" he exclaimed in consternation.

Before Viola could reply, Sister Sallie answered:

"Yes, she, having had varioloid in her youth, is not afraid to spend a few weeks with me at this delightfully pleasant resort."

The young girl's face reddened with indignation at this uncalled for and unexpected falsehood, and it was with considerable effort she controlled herself sufficiently to allow it to pass without contradiction. As they entered the house, the physician whispered softly to the lady leaning upon him:

"Would to God you, too, had had varioloid in your youth, and you would have been saved the dreadful trial before you; but be brave of heart," he added as he noticed her flushed cheek, "and all will yet be well."

CHAPTER XIX.

WE have not spoken of Coralie for a long time. We left her, if we recollect rightly, a little girl, recklessly wandering over hills and mountains, and boating, according to Sister Sallie, over dangerous rapids and deep falls. Yes, she was but a child when last we saw her, at least one in size and appearance, but not altogether in thought and reflection.

She never forgot that she was the cause, though the innocent one, of the banishment of Mary from her husband's home, and this fact stamped indelibly upon her young mind, the little instruction she had received concerning the truths of the Catholic religion, and in after life, when she saw base calumnies in circulation that were in direct opposition to the explanations she had received, her heart warmed towards that Church which St. Paul declared to be "The pillar and ground of truth," and promised that the gates of hell should never prevail against.

As she grew older, she borrowed from her friend Viola, of whom she was always devotedly fond, books containing the doctrine she had been prohibited hearing in her childhood, and she spent the time that is occupied by many in preparations for balls and pleasuring, forgetful of the end for which they are created, in searching for the truth, and at last she obeyed the command to "hear the Church," and became a devoted Catholic.

We find her once more at Glen Mary, and if we will take our way to the summer-house, where we were wont to resort, we will find her with her mother, engaged in deep and earnest conversation.

"Why, my child, my darling, can I believe my ears! That you wish to leave me, and for a convent?"

"I wish to leave you for God, for God alone, dearest mamma. Do not doubt my love. You cannot, you cannot."

"I'll try not, my darling," the mother said, gently stroking her daughter's hair, which had fallen loose in her excitement; "but is your religion so cruel that it would break asunder the nearest and the dearest ties, and would it oblige me to sacrifice my only child?"

"It does sever the ties of affection here, mother, in this transitory life, to bind them forever in our eternal home where, in never-ending bliss, we will live more and more united in the one great love of our heavenly Father which will absorb us there."

"But surely, Coralie, to attain that happiness it is not necessary for us to separate."

"Mother, darling, I feel that I am called to a higher life than the one that I am now leading. Sleeping or waking, I hear continually the command: 'Take up your cross and follow Me,' and believe me when I tell you that it is not easy for me to obey, and I have to pray continually for the grace to do so, and to frequently recall to mind the verse of Scripture that says: 'He that loves father or mother, sister or brother more than Me, is not worthy of Me.'"

"But, my precious child, are you not entirely too young to think of such a decided change in life?" said the poor mother coaxingly.

"Was I too young, mamma," returned the girl, smiling, "to have accepted Major Waldron when he complimented me enough to ask me to become his wife, and would not that have been a decided change of life, and yet you were very anxious for me to accept his offer.

"Why is it," she went on more earnestly, "that you would be willing for me to sacrifice my life, as you call it, to poor miserable man, and not be willing for it to be given to its Creator, who has promised that the 'Virgin shall follow the Lamb whithersoever he goeth.' Oh! mother, it has been two long, weary years since first I breathed this subject to you; you then said that if I would go out into the world for two years, and at the end of that length of time I still wanted to give it up, I could do so."

"Two years," the mother murmured more to herself than to her daughter, "is such a little while. What could you learn in that time of its attractions, its allurements, its pleasures. Tell me, child, what have you learned of this bright, beautiful world?"

"What knowledge I have gained of it?" replied Coralie quietly and thoughtfully. "Why, I have learned in those two little years as you term them, that man's standard of morality and God's standard differ as widely as heaven and earth are apart; that the world's virtues are wealth, arrogance, and dissimulation, its vices are truthfulness, modesty, and poverty; that the great end for which man was created is entirely forgotten and swallowed up in the search after a satisfactory settlement in life, and wealth easily acquired.

"And I have seen," she continued, sighing, "that the good are obliged to labor hard for safety, and literally to work out their salvation in fear and trembling, on account of the many and great temptations by which they are surrounded; and, mother," she added still more earnestly, "in opposition to all this, I found the world to be enchantingly beautiful, and captivating beyond words, and knew that it was not religion that made it so, and I felt all the time that if I loved the danger I must perish. I cannot live in the world, dear mother, for it is only by constant meditation that I can fully comprehend that life is but a preparation for death, and that it is not well for a soul, for which our Redeemer died upon a cross to save, should spend all its time to obtain comfort and ease, and to avoid sorrow."

"My dear, dear child! is this sacrifice necessary?" asked Mrs. Caroline, bursting into tears.

"Without making it, I feel that I could not save my soul, mother dearest."

A few months afterwards Coralie is received into a convent as a candidate, her beautiful long, braided hair, her greatest ornament and her poor mother's pride, was cut to suit the closely-fitting cap that novices wear, and Coralie, the bright, beautiful fascinating girl, is lost forever to vanity and to the world.

Lost forever to that world that she was so fitted to delight and adorn; lost, before the fresh bloom of youth and beauty had departed from her fair, sweet face; lost, before the sad experience which it always gives, had dimmed the brightness of her eye, or embittered the joyousness of her heart; in her youth, bloom, and health, she had voluntarily renounced it.

And now, one verse of Gerald Griffin's "Sister of Charity"—who, like our young friend Coralie, had "chosen the better part"—will describe in a few words the future of this brave girl, so for our reader's benefit we will insert it here:

"Her down-bed a pallet; her trinkets, a bead;
Her lustre, one taper, that serves her to read;
Her sculpture, the crucifix nailed by her bed;
Her paintings, one print of the thorned-crowned head;
Her cushion, the pavement that wearies the knees;
Her music, the psalm or the sigh of disease;
The delicate lady lives mortified there,
And the feast is forsaken for fasting and prayer."

Before ending the chapter, we feel tempted to insert also the last verse of that beautiful poem. God grant that the beauty, force, and truth with which it is written may cause one thoughtless mind to reflect, one ungrateful heart to love, and one poor soul lost in sin back to grace.

"Behold her, ye worldly! Behold her, ye vain!
Who shrink from the pathway of virtue and pain;
Who yield up to pleasure your nights and your days,
Forgetful of service, forgetful of praise!
Ye lazy philosophers—self-seeking men—
Ye fireside philanthropists, great at the pen,
How stands in the balance your eloquence weighed,
With the life and the deeds of that high-born maid?"

CHAPTER XX.

ONE November afternoon, as Annette was listening to Estelle reading Corinne, and patiently helping her to translate the beautiful story, Mrs. Fairfax suddenly proposed, as, with an impatient gesture, she threw down the book, "Let us order the carriage and ride. I cannot fix my mind on French to-day."

Annette assented, and shortly afterwards they were driving along the mountains and admiring their beauty, clothed, as they were, in their dress of many colors. Estelle said that their bright beauty reminded her of somebody's thought, she had forgotten whose, that the trees were nymphs blushing at the too near approach of winter's god, whom they knew would rob them of their grace and beauty, and then leave them bare and helpless to withstand his rude blasts of icy scorn.

"How beautiful it all is," answered Annette. "When I look around me on mornings like this, I often wonder how an atheist can see all this marvellous beauty without acknowledging God and saying with Moore:

> 'Where'er we turn, Thy glories shine,
> And all things fair and bright are Thine.'"

"But what surprises me even more than the atheist's want of faith," returned Estelle, "is the division amongst those who do believe and who call themselves Christians. Let us take ourselves for instance. Here we both are recognizing nature's great Architect, and yet, as regards our worship of Him, we differ so widely."

"The difference between us, ma'am, is not so great as you imagine it to be, for you have already acknowledged that our doctrine concerning the veneration of saints, pious images, confession, and other articles is misrepresented, but there is one article of faith that we do vitally disagree upon,* and that constitutes principally the difference between the Catholic and the Protestant."

"You mean," interrupted Estelle, "the doctrine of the Eucharist."

"Yes," she replied, "and you must confess, Mrs. Fairfax, that we Catholics have the best side of the argument, for our belief about this is strictly conformable to the words of Scripture."

"Do you mean to say," exclaimed Estelle in surprise, "that you take the literal sense of the Bible, and believe that you receive the true body and blood of Christ, when you partake of the bread and wine?"

"Yes, I believe that when I partake of the Blessed Sacrament, that I really and truly receive the body and blood of Christ," replied Annette.

"Please tell me exactly what you do think about this; I am all attention and am really curious to know how you can believe what you say you do."

"Why, I read in the sixth chapter of St. John that our Blessed Lord promised this divine mystery near one of the paschs before He instituted it, and declared Himself to be the Bread of Life, and that, if any man eat of it, he should live forever, and that when the Jews strove amongst themselves saying, 'How can this man give us His flesh to eat?' that our Lord answered with what was equivalent to an oath: "Amen, amen, I say unto you, except you eat of the flesh of the Son of man and drink His blood you shall not have life in you. He that eateth My flesh, and drinketh My blood hath everlasting life, and I will raise him up at the last day. For My flesh is meat indeed, and My blood is drink indeed.'

"Now it was not the Jews alone," continued Annette, "that took offense, but when some of His disciples heard it they said: 'This is a hard saying, who can hear it?' and they went back and walked with Him no more. And then I read that Jesus asked the twelve: 'Will you also go away?' and that Simon Peter answered Him: 'Lord, to whom shall we go? Thou hast the words of eternal life.' We Catholics believe that our loving, merciful Saviour would not have allowed His enemies, much less His friends, to desert Him to their own destruction, if He could have removed their difficulty by merely telling them that they were to receive in remembrance only, and would have contented Himself with simply asking His apostles if they would also leave. They were as incapable of comprehending the great mystery as others were, but they were assured that Christ's words were to be believed and made a generous act of faith, which all Christians should imitate."

"Have you any authority to prove that the early Christians believed this sacrament to be more than bread and wine?" asked Estelle.

"If I were to give you all the authority in proof of the real presence amongst the early Christians, I would speak for hours. St. Ignatius, an apostolic Bishop of the first century, speaking of some contemporaries says: 'They do not admit of Eucharist or oblation, because they do not believe the Eucharist to be the flesh of our Saviour Jesus Christ, who suffered for our sins.' St. Justin, St. Irenæus, St. Cyprian, Origen, and all the Fathers whose testimony was mighty enough to settle the canon of Scripture, affirm it. But I must content myself with only one or two quotations from them. Origen is authority for this one: 'Manna was formerly given as a figure, but now the flesh and blood of the Son of God is specifically given and is real food;' and St. Cyril of Jerusalem for this: 'Since Christ Himself affirms of His bread, "This is my body," who is so daring as to doubt it? And since He affirms, "This is my blood," who will deny that it is blood?' And, my dear Mrs. Fairfax, if we come down to later days, even your own Luther, whom the Protestant world in general is so fond of quoting, says: 'That you might as well try to destroy the Scriptures themselves as the literal sense of the Eucharist.'"

"It all puzzles me," replied Estelle, as she passed her small hand hurriedly across her brow.

"It was just as hard, my dear madam, for St. Peter to believe as it is for you now. Do as he did, go to Jesus, saying: 'Thou hast the words of eternal life;' accept the words of your Saviour, trust not the interpretation of man, and 'the Truth will set you free,'" said Annette, enthusiastically.

Here, either the sudden jump across the road of a deer, or the barking of the hounds in pursuit of the poor animal, caused the horses to bound forward, and they were soon running at a fearful rate down the road. A break in the harness threw the driver from his seat, and he was left wounded and bleeding upon the ground.

Annette caught the reins and tried with all the strength she was capable of to check the crazy steeds in their break-neck course, but to no purpose; each instant they ran faster and faster, until, to the occupants of the vehicle, they seemed to be flying. The road led down the side of a steep mountain—one full of peril, owing to the deep ravines on either side, for such a ride. Estelle sat motionless, paralyzed with terror; but at last, when the carriage nearly toppled over a precipice, she uttered a wild cry and clutching Annette convulsively screamed:

"Save me! Oh, save me!"

The cripple, who felt her hold on the reins to be useless dropped them, and throwing her arms around Estelle clasped her affectionately, exclaiming:

"Darling, God only can do that—ask Him!"

On the maddened horses ran at a fearful rate until at last, turning a sharp angle in the road, the carriage was thrown down a declivity of some twenty feet, taking the frightened women and the poor crazy animals with it to the bottom, where all lay a bleeding, stunned, and helpless mass.

CHAPTER XXI.

"SUSAN, is not that Dr. Fitzpatrick approaching?" asked Col. Graham of his wife as they were conversing one morning upon the piazza.

"I think so," she answered, after looking in the direction pointed out. "How I do hope it is," she went on, "for now we can learn exactly how poor Sister Sallie is."

As the horseman came nearer to view, and there was no mistaking the Doctor's sturdy form, she advanced hastily to the gate to meet him, followed by her husband.

After the usual salutations were over, Dr. Fitzpatrick told them that their sister was much improved; that her fever had abated considerably.

"The only trouble that I have now to contend with," he said in a serious tone, "is her mind. She is terribly dejected, so much so that I cannot account for it."

"Ah! poor thing, poor thing!" the Colonel murmured, as he threw the bridle reins to the servant who had come forward to take the Doctor's horse, "her affliction is dreadful, dreadful indeed, but cannot Viola cheer her, and make her look occasionally on the bright side?"

"I think Miss Williams is a great comfort to her," replied Dr. Fitzpatrick, "for frequently of late I catch them in deep and earnest conversation, and believe that since your sister's illness, she has grown wonderfully in her favor."

"I always believed Viola to be a good girl," Col. Graham said, and then added pleasantly: "Perhaps she is proselyting Sister Sallie like you are me, and it is theological disquisitions you interrupt when you go there."

The Doctor laughed, and said it might be so, when a scream from Mrs. Graham made both gentlemen start and turn towards her.

"Look, look!" she cried, as she pointed towards the mountain.

The sight that met their eyes was indeed an appaling one. Coming down the steep and dangerous descent were a pair of frightened horses, rushing madly on to their own destruction, dragging a carriage that was thrown upon its side. Piercing screams of terror were borne upon the air, which told the sad story that the vehicle was occupied.

On, on, came the crazy steeds, until they reached a precipice immediately in front of the horrified witnesses, then, as if made aware for the first time of the terrible fate they were hurrying to, with a mighty effort they threw themselves back on their haunches, but the effort at preservation came too late, the carriage was dashed over the brink. As it disappeared from view, Mrs. Graham screened her eyes, and grew white from fright. Col. Graham exclaimed:

"My God! my God! it is Fairfax's carriage."

Dr. Fitzpatrick uncovered his head, and lowered it at the same time and asked the "God of Mercy" to be merciful to the poor occupants. When he raised his head, nothing of the dreadful sight was to be seen, and for a moment the two gentlemen looked at each other in horror.

Col. Graham kindly led his terror-stricken wife into the house, and leaving hasty orders for assistance to be sent to him, again joined the Doctor, and they were soon at the scene of the catastrophe.

Both horses were found to be killed outright. The ladies were still alive. Whether their injuries were light or fatal, it was, as yet, impossible to say. They were found clasped in each others' arms, unconscious, and apparently lifeless. They were soon removed to the Glen, and Alfred apprized of his wife's danger. In a short time he was at her side, wild with grief and remorse. Forgotten now was all her wilfulness and temper, as he looked down upon the sad, white face resting upon his arm, lovelier in its grief than it ever was in joy. He thought only of her gentleness and patience whilst he was torturing her, and he repeated again those vows which he had once before made before God's minister, to both love and cherish her if she was but spared to him. But will she be spared?

Annette was soon restored to consciousness, and though fearfully agitated, was found to be unhurt, with the exception of some rather severe bruises and scratches. Dr. Fitzpatrick administered a soothing powder, and she was ordered to keep her room and remain perfectly quiet for a few days.

Estelle's case puzzled the Doctor. When she recovered from her swoon, she complained of no pain, and upon examination no bones were found to be broken; but she lay so white and still, that she seemed scarcely to be breathing.

Late that afternoon he was left alone in the library at Glen Mary. His thoughts seemed sad and deeply occupied, perhaps he was revolving some plan in his mind by which he could save that poor young wife, but it was evident from the expression of his face, that he had but little hope of doing so. A beautiful landscape, brought distinctly to view by a bright, full moon that threw silvery gleams over its grassy slopes and purple mountains, spread far out before him, and which seemed to be inviting admiration, was unnoticed.

After some time he arose from the window in which he was seated, and walked to the mantel where a photograph of Viola was resting. He returned to his seat, where the brilliant moonlight discovered each feature to his earnest gaze.

"Is it possible?" he soliloquized, as he looked upon the frank, lovely face of the picture, "that a face expressive of so much truth and honor, can cover only deceit, and want of feeling?"

He sighed heavily and, for the first time, looked out upon the night, and saw something of its beauty. He had scarcely done so when his attention was arrested by a door at the end of the room being stealthily and noiselessly opened, and a queer little figure entered. She held a lamp in one hand and a crutch in the other. For an instant she paused, and turned the light so that she could take a survey of the apartment.

As she ran her eye rapidly around the room, Dr. Fitzpatrick involuntarily shrunk back further behind the curtain, and was hidden from sight. Satisfied that she was alone, she crossed over to where a portrait was hanging, and regarded it earnestly. Her presence seemed to have a mesmeric effect upon the Doctor. He could not remove his glance from the little creature, as she leaned on her crutch and held the lamp so that its rays would reach the picture. As she threw her head further back to inspect the portrait still more closely, heavy masses of white hair became uncoiled, rolled over her shoulders and down her back, almost reaching the floor.

Apparently the escape of her snowy tresses was unnoticed, and to the astonished eyes fastened upon her, she appeared like the inhabitant of another world. Her cheeks were white and thin, her features sharp and shrunken, and in her large, dark eye was an expression of so much sorrow, combined with such deep, unutterable love that Dr. Fitzpatrick brushed a tear of sympathy off his cheek, and dropped his head in his hands in thought and perplexity. There was certainly something in that poor little grief-stricken face that was familiar.

Why was he reminded of the girl he had been thinking of when she entered? He had recognized her at once as Mrs. Fairfax's French governess, that he had left too ill to rise an hour before; but still there was something he could not fathom. As a groan of anguish escaped her, he raised his head and still more closely scanned her, concluding as he did so, that it was sorrow, not years that had aged her, and for the first time he remembered that he was guilty of a great rudeness to be thus observing her, and she unconscious of his presence; the thought of his ungentlemanliness confused him so that, for a moment, he was uncertain how to act, but in another instant he had decided.

"I'll try it," he said under his breath; "for if I'm correct in my suspicion it will but prove it, otherwise it can do no harm."

As he said it, there arose on the air a long, loud, clear, lugubrious sound that would have startled sterner stuff than the queer little woman was made of; and as the shrill voice burst suddenly upon her ear, with a wild cry of affright, she dropped both the lamp and the crutch, and went as fast as her stiffened limbs would carry her from the apartment.

"Poor little woman!" Dr. Fitzpatrick exclaimed compassionately, as he walked towards the lamp which was not extinguished by the fall. "I did not think to frighten her so, and such a hasty retreat for a cripple, without a crutch," he added smiling. "By Jove! I thought it was his picture," he went on, as he raised the light and scanned the features of the portrait above it; and now a strange transformation took place in the rather dignified gentleman. He whistled, hopped and jumped like a child wild with delight, and a looker-on would have thought that he was either beside himself with joy, or fast recovering his long lost boyishness.

CHAPTER XXII.

LET us go to Oakland and find out what those earnest conversations can be about that Dr. Fitzpatrick said occurred so often between Mrs. Graham and her nurse. As we enter, it will sadden us to find the poor sufferer with her eyes closely shaded, her hands tightly bandaged, moaning and groaning as she tosses to and fro upon her bed of pain.

"Oh! Viola," she is murmuring as we go in, "do you really think there is hope for all, and that God will forgive a life regardless of Him altogether?"

"Indeed I do," the pale girl beside her answered. "Remember, it was to save sinners that His only Son's precious blood was shed."

"But you do not know how wicked, how awfully wicked I am," the invalid said shuddering.

"Which of us," was gently asked, "in the sight of God will be perfect?"

"That thought, girl, only makes my despair greater; for if you and poor Mary are not perfect in his sight, what a defiled thing I must be. Oh! it is no use, no use; it is too late, too late for me to repent."

"It is never too late to repent, as long as life is granted us. Come, say this little prayer, 'Lord have mercy on me,'" said Viola, earnestly and coaxingly.

"No, no, I cannot, must not call upon Him now, who, in health and strength, I would not even think of," the sufferer answered excitedly.

"Mrs. Graham," Viola spoke in a sadly solemn voice, "no matter how great your offences have been, you are now committing one greater than any, or all of them combined."

"Enlighten me," the conscience-stricken woman answered, "for I do not know how I am offending in being afraid to go to Him, as you tell me I must do."

"Why, are you not, by refusing, limiting the mercy of the good God? That is your sin. Oh! Mrs. Sallie, do not do that. If your soul in His sight is as red as scarlet, He can and will make it whiter than snow. Remember the dying thief; like him, one little appeal from your heart for mercy will save you. Make it, make it," Viola begged imploringly.

"I cannot now; wait until after brother comes, and when you have heard all that I wish to say to him; if you can then think there is mercy for such a miserable wretch, I will ask for it."

"Well, here he comes now," cried Viola, as, at that moment, she caught sight of the Graham carriage approaching.

In a short time Col. Graham was shown into the sick room, accompanied by Dr. Fitzpatrick. After partially answering the many questions concerning her condition, asked by both gentlemen, the sick woman said:

"I sent for you, brother, for I wished, before I

died, to make a confession, and to restore, as far as I am able, the peace and harmony of Glen Mary."

Here she was interrupted by her physician.

"My dear madam, there is no danger of your dying; you are almost convalescent now; so pray don't say in our presence what only the fear of death would occasion, for you might regret it hereafter."

"For once you are mistaken," the invalid answered; "I feel certain that my end will be soon; but even if you are right, I have felt the awfulness of the nearness of death, and if life is granted me, I intend to make it very different from my past. I must relieve my mind of the load upon it, and make restitution, as far as I can. Oh! if George were but here so that I could tell him all! Do you know," she said excitedly, raising up and looking in the direction of her brother-in-law, "that I have been a curse to you and your household, that I am the cause of your son's blighted life? Yes, the thought of being supplanted by his fair, young wife was agony to me, and I resolved to get rid of her.

"I made him," she went on in a higher key, "drive her away, and it was I that carefully prevented her whereabouts ever being known, and intercepted, for over a year, her letters of love and entreaty to be allowed to come back, and wrote the cruel answers that must have caused her poor heart to bleed. Can you forgive me?" she asked in an hysterical voice, and she tried to raise her bandaged hands towards him with a gesture of touching entreaty.

"Poor creature, poor creature! her mind wanders," the Colonel whispered to Viola.

"No, no," answered Sallie, "I am perfectly sane; am I not, Doctor?"

"Yes, perfectly," he answered sadly, which made Col. Graham groan aloud.

"Where can she be found?" he asked in a husky voice, with lips that had lost all color.

"That I do not know, for two years ago she disappeared from where I placed her, and being unable even to trace her, I fear—" here she stopped and shuddered.

"You fear that she has destroyed herself?" interrupted Col. Graham.

"Yes," she falteringly said.

At this answer the Colonel seemed completely overcome. He bowed his head upon his hands to hide the large tears that were rolling down his cheeks.

Viola, although she felt for the poor penitent, could not repress a feeling of revulsion, and was almost unable to control herself. She involuntarily glanced towards Dr. Fitzpatrick, and, much to her surprise, saw that he was smiling, and she thought, as she had once before, that the grief of others was only amusement to him.

As her eye was resting on him full of reproach, he looked up and caught the expression, and from the bright color that overspread his face, she saw that he knew of what she was thinking.

For awhile all were silent, busy with their own thoughts.

The silence was broken by the invalid saying in a pathetic voice:

"You have not given me your forgiveness yet, brother."

"We must forgive as we hope to be forgiven," Col. Graham answered gravely, whilst he gently stroked her poor, bandaged hands. As he spoke, big tears stole down her face, and sighs shook her wasted frame. After awhile she turned towards Dr. Fitzpatrick, saying:

"You and Viola come nearer, for you two have much to forgive, and Viola more than all; for I deprived her of her mother's dying blessing, and she the consolation of having her child present in her last hour. Can you pardon that?"

"I do," answered the sobbing girl. "You must not let that worry you any more, and my mother forgives you too," she softly whispered, "and is praying for you in Heaven."

For an instant a smile radiated the poor disfigured face, and then she continued.

"But that is not all, Viola; I discovered your love, even before it was known to yourself, and vowed you should never—"

"Oh! Mrs. Graham," interrupted the now blushing and painfully embarrassed girl, "say no more, please, *please*, do not; I forgive you all, everything."

"This is no time for concealment, girl. I must tell all that weighs upon me, so that in the little time that's left me to live, I may make my peace with God."

"No, no, please keep silent," pleaded Viola, whilst she gently placed her hand over the invalid's mouth.

"Well, I will not embarrass you further, but won't you tell me, Dr. Fitzpatrick, that you, too, pardon me?" she asked in a tremulous voice.

"I have nothing to pardon," he answered softly, "but as your physician, I must insist upon your not speaking again, and," looking towards Viola, "upon her being kept perfectly quiet." Here he made a sign to Col. Graham, and they both started to leave the chamber.

"Oh! brother," cried Mrs. Graham as he arose to depart, "promise me one thing more! You will not, you must not, refuse to send for George. I cannot rest, either in this world or in the next, until I have told him how cruelly I have injured him, and obtained his forgiveness."

Col. Graham knew not how to answer. He disliked very much to refuse what he considered a dying request, but he knew to bring his son home now would be but to add to his wretchedness, for he would learn additional particulars of the dreadful cruelty that drove his poor young wife to destruction. He turned to Dr. Fitzpatrick for advice, and, like Viola, was surprised at the expression of his face.

"You should send for your son at once," the Doctor answered. "It is but right that he should know of every circumstance relating to his wife."

And so the Colonel gave the required promise.

Contrary to Sister Sallie's prediction, she did not

die, but lived for many years afterwards a useful and contented life, though forever despoiled of her wondrous beauty. And she would not, until old and enfeebled, make her home again at Glen Mary.

Her repentance was sincere and heartfelt, and she often acknowledged the goodness and mercy that brought her within the shadow of the tomb, thus making her fully realize the terribleness of a sinner appearing in the presence of the great God.

She always said that Viola was the instrument that her Redeemer used to cause her conversion. That her hard, cruel heart was first touched by a ray of heavenly grace, when she saw that beautiful religion, that teaches to love your enemies, to do good to those who hate you, and forgive those who have injured you, exemplified in her.

The loss of her great beauty was another source of thankfulness, for she well knew the danger of being beautiful, and was glad that she could no longer be vain or foolish. We will here, for the present, bid her adieu, though we would much rather renew our acquaintance with her in her new character, than to dwell upon her past.

CHAPTER XXIII.

MRS. FAIRFAX did not improve. It was becoming evident to all now that she was in great danger.

When Dr. Fitzpatrick was appealed to by the almost broken-hearted husband, his opinion was that she had suffered some internal injury that medicine could not reach. She was still unable to be removed to Dunreath Abbey, and each day, as it passed, took away some of her strength and bloom.

Yes, Estelle was sinking, and sinking rapidly. Annette never left her, and confined as she was to the invalid's room, she knew nothing of the joyous welcome going on down stairs, to the long absent son, who had returned at last, after three years' weary wandering in foreign lands, to his childhood's home, to the fond embrace of loving parents, to—but for one fatal remembrance—peace and rest.

Alfred knew that he had arrived, and waited impatiently for the happy greetings to be over, the thousand and one questions asked and answered, before going down to bring him to his wife, hoping that travel, and the experience it entails, may have acquainted him with a case similar to hers.

Why do we despair when there is much of hope before us, and why hope when there is nothing but the blackness of despair in our path? What strange beings we are!

Estelle, who had been slumbering, opened her eyes and asked Annette whose step that was approaching with Alfred's. Receiving no answer, she turned her head, and was shocked to see a strange, frightened look in her face, and that she was deadly pale.

She was trying to speak, but her white lips essayed no sound. As the steps came nearer, she looked imploringly at Estelle as if she was asking for protection, and muttered brokenly:

"Has he come? Has he come?"

Just then the door opened, and Mr. Fairfax and George entered, followed by Dr. Fitzpatrick, who was just in time to catch the little woman as she was falling in a swoon to the floor.

"Poor little thing, she has been such a careful nurse, that she has exhausted herself," said Alfred, by way of explanation, to George.

"No, no!" cried Estelle, who was fearfully excited, "it is not exhaustion; not that, not that! Look at her, husband; look at her, George, and see —see if she is—or am I dreaming?" and she sank back on her pillow completely overcome.

"See if she's who?" exclaimed George excitedly.

"*Your wife!*" gravely said Dr. Fitzpatrick, as he laid the unresisting form of the cripple in his arms.

"Mary, Mary, my darling, my wife! have I found you at last? O great God! I thank Thee for this mercy!" cried George, as he kissed repeatedly the sad, white face on his arm.

Gradually she revived, but before she recovered

consciousness entirely, she seemed to know, by some blessed intuition, of the happy change in her existence. As she opened her eyes, she murmured:

"Does my husband really want me?"

"Want you, beloved? Does he want sunshine and life? Does he want everything that's noble, that's good, that's beautiful? Does he want to be truly and really blessed? If he wants all this, then he wants you, my beloved!"

The bright smile that illumined her face as he spoke made it lose years of its greyness and age; but suddenly it lost all its brightness and looked more haggard than ever before, and she tried to withdraw herself from him, exclaiming:

"Oh! I had forgotten that other one! that other one, where is she?"

"What other one?" George asked in affright, fearing her mind wandered.

"Why, the one that stands between you and me—that one the law calls your wife—the one that went with you to Europe!"

"Why, are you crazy, Mary? I have never had but one wife, and that is the one that I now hold in my arms."

"Father in Heaven, I thank Thee!" the young wife ejaculated. "This is more happiness than I can bear!" and again she fainted.

Whilst the husband is restoring her with kisses and happy tears, we will look at Estelle, who, much to her physician's surprise, is wonderfully calm. Her room is rapidly filling now, for from mouth to mouth, throughout the house, the joyous tidings are being borne: "The young mistress, the lost wife, has been found."

"You might as well try to stay the wind," Dr. Fitzpatrick remarked to Alfred, who was solely annoyed for fear the excitement might injure Estelle. "There is no help for it; she is standing it bravely, let it blow over of itself."

The poor husband felt like it was years before it did so, but at last the wonder, the excitement, the happy greetings all belonged to the past; but the joy over the lost one being found is as great as ever.

Mary is seated between her husband and Estelle, who insisted upon hearing Mary's story, holding a hand of each, with Dr. Fitzpatrick, the Colonel, and his wife near.

We will give her story in her own words, leaving out the frequent interruptions of her intensely interested listeners.

"The night I left here," she commenced in a voice husky with emotion, "is almost a blank in my memory. All that I can remember about it is, that when I recovered reason I was roaming about in a fearful tempest, and so exhausted that it was with difficulty that I could walk at all; but I persevered and went on, though with no definite object in view. I cared little whither I went; all the country was the same to me, as I was unknown and knew no one. At length I was so weary that I felt that I could go no further, when a long, wild flash of lightning showed me you, George, directly in my path. I have often thought of it since, and still believe it was no hallucination of the brain, for I saw you as distinctly as I ever did in my life. You looked both pale and frightened. Though flash after flash followed in quick succession, I could see you no more, and a nervous fear, which added to the horror of my situation, took possession of me.

"Oh! it was an awful, awful night. The waters that were rushing down the mountain sides were so strong that I was often taken off my feet and thrown to the ground, whilst the drops that were falling so big and fast on my head almost crushed me with their weight. Towards morning, overcome by exhaustion and unable to proceed further, I felt that death was inevitable, and prayed for mercy for my soul I remember nothing more. When I again opened my eyes I thought for awhile that I was here at home, and had just waked up from a distressing dream, for sitting near, and gazing intently at me, was Aunt Sallie. At first she was the only object in the room that I could distinguish; but as my eyes grew stronger, I saw that there was another woman there who was a stranger to me, and that the objects in the apartment were not familiar, and then, as the certainty of my trouble came over me, I cried out in pain and affright.

"'You are not afraid of me, surely, Mary, you are not?' softly asked Mrs. Graham, as she came over to where I was lying, and gently stroked my forehead. 'Ah! I see that you are,' she said, reproachingly, as I did not answer. 'You see now, Mrs. Lawson, how unjust this poor child is to me. She is the only one at the Glen who will not look upon me as a friend. Well, Mary, if I restore you to your husband will you believe in me then?'

"'Only do that,' I implored, 'and I will bless you every day, every hour of my life. And oh!' I went on, 'you can, you can! for what you advise is always done. Only give me back my husband, and I will prove my thankfulness by a life of gratitude.'

"She smiled, saying: 'All I can do for you, child, shall be gladly done; but come, you must remain quiet. Are you in any pain?'

"So great was my mental agony that I had not thought before of my bodily suffering; but now as she, by her promise, had eased the burthen upon me, I felt that I was suffering physically also, and for twelve long months I never rose from that bed of pain.

"The exposure of that night had brought on acute rheumatism, and that accounts for those crutches," she said, glancing towards them.

"During all that time Mrs. Lawson carefully nursed me, and Aunt Sallie came often. But although she brought me many delicacies, and was very kind every time she came, I dreaded her coming, for she always brought me one of those cruel letters from you, George, that invariably made me worse for days afterwards.

"I remember so well the first evening that I was able to sit up. They seated me in a window from which stretched a lovely landscape of grassy slope and bluish mountains, and for the first time for over a year I was able to look out upon the beauties of nature. The world looked so bright, the birds sang so sweetly, that I felt some sunshine steal into my heart, and I began to grow hopeful, and almost feel happy once more. That morning I had written you a long letter, telling of my affliction, and begging you, as a physician, in charity to come and relieve my pain. I hoped much from it, for it was different from any that I had ever written you before; in no other had I ever mentioned my suffering, and knowing your tender sympathy for pain, I thought you would come to relieve me, perhaps would pity me and love me again.

"As I sat there hoping much from our meeting, which I felt would take place in a little while, I saw a servant from Glen Mary cross the yard and hand Mrs. Lawson two notes, one of which proved to be for me, the other for herself. Through some mistake of Aunt Sallie's—who wrote them—they were misdirected. Mrs. Lawson's was addressed to me, and mine to her. It was that note, my dear George, that changed my brown locks to these of snow. It commenced by begging the woman to take good care of me, and if possible to keep the dreadful truth from my ears; for, it went on to say, if she should hear he has obtained a divorce, it would distress her beyond measure; but for her to learn that he is on the eve of starting with his new bride to Europe, would kill her outright. From my heart I pity the poor, young thing. I could read no more. Though I did not lose my senses, I was powerless to either speak or move.

"Mrs. Lawson, who, whilst I read, was looking

out the window, now turned towards me, and as she did so, she screamed so loud that her husband came running in to learn the cause of her fright.

"'What is the matter with her,' she asked, pointing towards me; 'she looks as if she were turned into stone, and, my God! her hair is changing white!'

"The man poured the contents of a pitcher of ice water into my face, but as that did not cause me to move, he caught me by the shoulders and shook me violently. I was ill for many weeks. As I regained strength, all hope being dead within me, I felt it incumbent to do something for a living. About this time Aunt Sallie, who still visited me, brought me some papers to read. In looking over them I saw an account of the duel between Alfred and George, and learned from it that I was believed to be dead. The editor added to the notice that the place suffered no loss in losing me, for, like my mother Eve, I was at the bottom of all the trouble in the county. In one of them I saw your advertisement, Estelle, for a French teacher. Remembering my promise to your mother to be with you as much as possible, and knowing that I was competent to instruct you in French, I thought of applying for it. At first I was undecided whether to go to you and contradict the belief of my death or not. My changed appearance, the knowledge that you believed me dead, what the editor had said of my being the cause of so much trouble, and the fear of causing more determined me. And besides, a divorced woman has every cause to wish to avoid publicity. My eyes still being very weak I bought the glasses, that completed my disguise, and applied for the situation, taking my middle name, which is after my mother's youngest sister, Annette Berdeau.

"Since then, dear Estelle," she added touchingly, turning towards her, "you have made me as contented as my sad lot would let me be anywhere, and I felt that in being with you I was but fulfilling a sacred promise to the dead. George, the story of your second marriage I never heard contradicted until you did it this morning!"

Her lips quivered, happy tears filled her eyes, and she bowed her head upon her husband's shoulder and wept aloud. There was not a dry eye in all the room.

CHAPTER XXIV.

ONE morning, about a week after Mary was found, Estelle called Alfred to her bedside and said:
"I am going away from you dear husband; lean closer to me"—and she held up her poor, thin arms to embrace him—"I cannot die in peace until you promise what I have so often implored."

"My—my darling! my love! do not speak thus. You cannot, you shall not leave me," and he clasped her convulsively in his arms.

"But don't you promise me, Alfred," she said with tears in her eyes; "or do you," she added, "refuse your wife's dying request?"

"I refuse you nothing, my beloved, my life, my soul! Do with me as you will, only do not leave me, but live so that I may atone to you for the past. Oh! how carefully will I guard thee, darling; how I will cherish and protect thee; no rough hand shall ever cause thee pain; no rude word will ever mar thy peace, nor unkind act shall ever wound thy heart. All will be peace, joy, and love for evermore, if you will live, darling, for your Alfred's sake."

As he pleaded, his large, luminous eyes grew heavy with unshed tears.

"Poor Alfred, my poor, dear Alfred! Will you miss me then so much?"

"Miss you, precious love? If you go from me, the light of my life will go out. Oh, Estelle! you have never known how madly I have worshipped thee; how I gloried in your rare beauty; how I revelled in the thought that my wife was not like other men's, but vastly superior. There was a time, a dark, dark time my darling, when I thought that I was not necessary to your happiness, and a suicidal frenzy took possession of me. It was not the fear of a dreadful hereafter that stayed my self-destroying hand, but the knowledge that I could never see thee more. It was then that I took to drink, not that I loved the wine cup, but that I could drown my sorrow in it. Oh! my wife—I say it not reproachfully — you could have made me anything you wished."

She sighed heavily, and nestled her white face closer to him.

"My pride, my vanity, my foolishness were great, dear Alfred; but greater than all was my suffering, when I saw their effect upon you, darling, and God only knows how I have prayed for this hour, when I could tell of my repentance. It is true, it has come late, but He doeth all things well, and it is only in mercy and love that He deals with us. Husband," she went on, "I had a dream once. I thought I carried in my hand two precious jewels, brighter than the sun, though tarnished in places. Heaven's Queen told me they were our souls—mine and yours, dear Alfred—and that they might shine for all eternity in the Great King's crown of glory, if we did but remove the spots. By resignation to my early death, just as I have regained your affections, I hope to erase mine, for that King only knows how I suffer in leaving you, or how bright, bright, this world is now to me. But life is granted you, love, to remove yours, and you will, my darling!"

As she finished speaking, she raised his hand and gently caressed it, whilst strong sobs convulsed his frame.

Here Mary entered. She started as she noticed the poor wife's agitation, and softly reproached her for exciting herself so much. Her words recalled Alfred to himself, and he instantly mastered his feeling, wondering as he did so, how he could have risked his darling's safety by exciting her so. Mary, feeling sorry for him, gently dismissed him, saying:

"I will stay here whilst you take some rest."

Mr. Fairfax did not oppose his wife's wish to die a Catholic; he rather preferred that religion, he said, though he had to be almost forced from the room whilst the priest was hearing her confession. To leave her an instant was intolerable agony, though he suffered intensely whilst with her, noting the many changes for the worse that were rapidly taking place; still it was far better than absence. The little while he could call her his, seemed to have taken wings, it was flying away so fast, and his great love was miserly of moments that were passing away forever.

The few minutes it required the dying penitent to make her peace with God, seemed to the distracted husband hours of torture, and when Dr. Fitzpatrick advised him to remain away so that his wife could have perfect quiet, he begged so hard for permission to return, promising that he would neither speak nor move, that it was impossible for the compassionate physician to prevent his doing so.

For a day and night he took a position in the room, where he was unseen by the one that he would have died to have saved. Refusing to eat or to sleep, never moving a muscle, sat that repentant husband, satisfied with an occasional glimpse of the idol of his life that was so fast gliding from him. Sometimes when she slumbered he would steal noiselessly to her side to see the beloved face once more. One of the times as he gazed upon her with a world of agony in his face, she opened her eyes and caught the glance.

"My poor, poor Alfred!" she feebly murmured, and held up her wasted hands.

This simple action seemed to awaken the poor, grief-stricken husband to all his guilt, overpowering him with its force, and he fell insensible at her side.

When he was restored to consciousness, they were raising Estelle to receive her God. Mary fastened a snow-white veil, symbolical of purity, on her head. A new beauty shone in her face that was never there before, as it expressed the rapture and thanksgiving that were filling her heart at the reception of her Lord. The solemnity of the scene, and the knowledge it gave that the end had come, again overpowered the suffering Alfred. With a wild cry and arms extended, as if to keep her from going, he rushed towards her and again fell unconscious to the floor.

But his distress did not distract Estelle from her new found love. Perhaps, as she lay there apparently unconscious of everything, she was entreating for him the pity and grace that he needed. Presently she opened her eyes and slowly raising her thin, white hand to her breast, murmured softly:

"Let him rest here."

Gently they raised him, and tenderly placed his head upon her shoulder. As he slowly revived, she sweetly said:

"I'm not afraid to leave thee now, dear husband, for when I'm in Heaven, I'll obtain for you all that you need."

Her eyelids closed, and her head sank. Death was gently approaching. They knelt around her, and the gray-haired pastor commenced the prayers for the departing:

"Farewell, young wife, it is well for you to depart now! Stay not here to strive with trouble and temptation, that will but thicken with advancing years, when Heaven is inviting you to joy and to rest."

Again her lips move.

"Alfred, do you forgive me?"

"Yes, yes, my darling. I have nothing to forgive," he answered hoarsely.

She smiled and looked up at him with eyes full of gratitude and love, and then spoke for the last time:

"Mary, sing *Ave Sanctissima*."

Mary, commanding herself, complied, and when her soft, sweet voice reached

> "Whisper of Heaven to Faith,
> Sweet Mother, sweet Mother, hear,"

Estelle lowered her head upon her husband's arm and went to sleep.

CHAPTER XXV.

"SISTER Sallie refuses to return to us, wife," said Col. Graham, a few weeks after Estelle was laid to rest. "I have just received a note from her, positively declining to come. I thought of riding over there this morning, to try to persuade her that it was useless and foolish in her to so absent herself. Will you accompany me, Dr. Fitzpatrick? I wish you would, and as we ride along we can discuss your Pope's infallibility, that we were speaking of last night."

"Let me go also," said George; "not that I care to hear your discussion, but to persuade poor Aunt Sallie that she has suffered enough, and must come back to us."

"If you really wish to go, my son, I will order the carriage; your doing so will give me infinite pleasure, for I can never lose sight of the fact that Sallie was my brother's loved and honored wife."

"Don't forget your promise about Viola, husband; remember she is also to make Glen Mary her home," spoke Mrs. Graham.

"I don't know about that," interrupted George; "there is a gentleman who objects seriously to Glen Mary being her home."

"What! you don't wish Viola to live here! Why, George!" exclaimed the Colonel and his wife in a breath.

"I'm not the gentleman," answered the young doctor pleasantly, nodding as he spoke towards Dr. Fitzpatrick, whilst his eyes winked with merriment. His significant nod caused a laugh at the doctor's expense, and considerably embarrassed him, and he did not recover his confusion until they were fairly started for Oakland.

The road traversed one of those luxuriant valleys that are scattered here and there throughout a mountainous country, like oases in a desert. Rich, heavy grass, the natural growth of the soil, spread far out on either side. One of those perpetual mountain breezes was causing it to rise and fall in large, bright waves, that were beautiful to look upon, whilst the gentle rustling amongst its blades soothed like soft, low music; and its hedge of purple mountain, upon which the evening sun was scintillating its golden beams, added to the grandeur of the scene, and made the landscape appear one of surpassing beauty.

"I have gazed upon Italia in all her glory of natural wonders; I have felt Vesuvius' breath of fire, and looked in awe and wonder upon her forked tongues of flame; I have witnessed the splendor of her sunsets, and the majesty of her moons, and my very soul seemed stirred within me; yet the loveliness of these valleys surpasses them all," spoke Dr. Graham enthusiastically, as he pointed to the waves of grass. Both gentlemen agreed with him that it was a lovely scene, and then rode on in silence for some moments, when the Colonel suddenly looked towards Dr. Fitzpatrick, saying:

"Now for your explanation, sir."

"First you must give one to me," replied the Doctor. "Now tell *concisely* and *distinctly* what you think our meaning is when we call our Chief Bishop infallible?"

"Why, of course, you mean that he is incapable of sin," answered Col. Graham.

"Your answer is exactly what I supposed it would be," returned the Doctor. "Pardon me, Col. Graham," he added gravely, "when I say that many of us speak the English language and do not understand the words we utter."

"Well, pray enlighten me, sir, for I cannot see what other definition you can give to the word infallible," the Colonel said rather warmly.

"Excuse me for interrupting you," interposed Dr. Graham, "but I think I can see your mistake, sir," he said, addressing his father. "You have confounded the words *infallible* and *impeccable*. As I understand it, infallibility is freedom from error, and impeccability inability to sin; am I right, Dr. Fitzpatrick?"

"Yes, sir; and it is simply the confounding of those two words that principally makes our dogma of the infallibility of the Pope such a bugbear to the Protestant world. Now, there is no Catholic, be he ever so ignorant, that would dare call the Pope impeccable, whilst he would be willing to give his life to prove his infallibility."

"In what does his infallibility consist?" questioned the Colonel.

"Why, only as regards matters of faith and morals, and in expounding to the unlearned and unstable, who wrest the Scripture to their own destruction, and in this we do not differ so materially from you."

"How is that?" spoke up the Colonel.

"Why," answered Dr. Fitzpatrick, "in the Protestant world there is a multiplicity of popes, whilst in the Catholic world there is but one. I am fortunate enough to number amongst my most intimate friends," he continued, "many Protestants of various denominations, and each of them has his own pope. Upon those passages of Scripture that are hard to be understood, one will receive the expoundings of one preacher, one of another, and so on, until popes are multiplied to a numberless amount."

Here the stoppage of the carriage in front of Oakland prevented any further discussion, and the occupants upon alighting were shown immediately into Mrs. Graham's presence. Viola was not present, and some little time elapsed before she made her appearance. Though they used every argument that their ingenuity could devise, Sallie could not be prevailed upon to go back to Glen Mary.

"No, no, brother," she would answer to all his entreaties to return, "not yet awhile. Wait until peace and happiness have long resumed their sway there, and the feeling of pity you all express will not be mingled with one of reproach—then I will thankfully go back and spend my old age in contentment within its hospitable walls."

With this answer Col. Graham had to be satisfied. Viola, at the earnest solicitation of the whole Graham family, consented to make her home there, as she had no relatives, and but few friends, besides that family.

About three months after she had become a member of the family at the Glen, she was alone one evening in the back parlor, going over in thought the events of the last few years of her life. She arose from her position near the window, opened the piano, and began, in a melancholy voice, to sing a little song, which she improvised as she played:

> Yes, I have been thinking to-day,
>   Of the joys and the sorrows of the past;
> How merrily glided each moment away,
> How gladsome, how joyous, how bright seemed each day,
>   Till the years of my youth were past.
>
> Ah! God was good to me then,
>   And His love surrounded my path;
> He gave me a heart that was as light and free
> As the song of a bird, or the hum of a bee;
>   But all that has gone with the past.
>
> And God is good to me now,
>   Though the stroke of His rod is hard;
> For I have felt the depth of the woe,
> The dreadful pain which all must know,
>   When a loved one sleeps under the sod.
>
> So I have been thinking to-day,
>   And this lesson I've learned from the past,
> That the joys and sorrows we live through here,
> Make us tire of earth and for Heaven prepare,
>   Where our joys forever will last.

"My poor child, are you then so sad?" said a kind voice, whilst a hand was laid caressingly upon her head.

She started, turned, and confronted Dr. Fitzpatrick.

"Why, I thought I was all alone," she said, not knowing exactly how to recover herself.

"And so you were, child, until your plaintive voice drew me from the verandah, where I was seated. By the way, whose reflections were those you were singing so mournfully?"

"I must claim them for my own," she answered, rising and returning to the open window, which she had vacated a short time before.

He followed and drew his chair beside her.

"Viola," he said, after a moment's hesitation, "is it not time for you to return to your own bright, natural self? It is not natural, my child, to repine unceasingly."

"I do not," she answered in a tremulous voice; "I am endeavoring all the time to banish sadness."

"Then I'm afraid you are not a skilful manœuverer," he said; then added pleasantly: "May I turn Gypsy for a little while, and tell you why you do not succeed?"

"Oh, yes," she answered, as she playfully held out her hand for the lines and cross lines to be examined and criticised.

"Well, in the first place," commenced the Gypsy, in a mock-solemn voice, "the lady is in love, and will not admit her lover into her presence."

"For once, a Gypsy is mistaken," Viola said, interrupting him. "There is no one whose presence I deny."

"How then can young Rogers' absence be accounted for?" asked the Gypsy, forgetful of his assumed tone.

"Young Rogers!" repeated the girl in amazement; "why I know no such person."

"Why, were you not with a family of that name in the summer of 185—, that you passed at the —— springs?"

"I don't think I know amongst all my acquaintances even one single person of that name; and I am very sure that whilst I staid at the springs, I did not know the family you speak of," said Viola, still surprised; "for," she went on, "the proprietor and his wife were the only persons there we knew well enough to recognize by even the most distant bow. My poor mother was too great a sufferer for me to leave her to form acquaintances."

Dr. Fitzpatrick's looks showed his great astonishment, but he said nothing, except to mutter something about having been deceived, which the lady near him could not catch.

For some time neither spoke; then drawing his chair still closer to Viola, and lowering his voice, the Doctor said gently:

"Little girl, do you know that I have deeply wronged you, and that you have much to forgive in me?"

"Much to forgive in you?" she questioned.

"Yes; but before I explain, let me give you a short history of one of your friends. A gentleman well known to you, and who is now in the sere and yellow leaf of life, was, when first grown to manhood, engaged to a fair young girl whom he had known and loved from infancy. Edgar Poe's "Annabel Lee" describes better his love for her than I can tell it you. Yes, his love was more than a love, and it must have been offensive to the Creator of affection, for He called the gentle creature this man claimed as his own, to His bright and happy home above, and left him desolate indeed. Years sped on, and still the man's heart loved not again, and he thought the chord, so sweetly touched in his youth, was hushed to vibrate no more, until suddenly and unexpectedly it was played upon by a maiden, whose every look and gesture reminded him of his long lost love. His youth, for awhile, returned to this old man, and he indulged as of yore in air castles, and would dream of a happy home, a loving wife, and of all that makes earth blest; but, alas! he was again doomed to misery—for he discovered, or thought he discovered, that the maid that had restored to him his youth, resembled his lost darling only in form and appearance, for he was made to believe that the living one was both heartless and deceitful. This belief killed, for the second time, the heart that could love so much, and he coldly, nay rudely, repulsed every effort the girl made to gain his friendship. But, Viola, he has found out his mistake, and once again his heart is alive to love, and he wishes to take and to cherish there, the girl he had so loved and so wronged. Can he do it?"

Viola looked up; the eyes she encountered told her more than the words to which she had been listening; they made her heart throb violently. She essayed to speak, but words failed her. At last tears came to her relief, but they were happy tears—and just then the great, round moon stole from behind a cloud, and gave a smile of approval down upon the lovers.

CONCLUSION.

THE chapel bells are ringing; they peal out clear and merrily on the air this clear, balmy, autumnal morning. We must obey the summons, and with the family from Glen Mary repair thither and witness again two brides breathe their vows of fidelity. One is the bride of man, the other is the bride of heaven. Coralie advances to the altar first, and in a soft, silvery voice, repeats the words that bind her to God alone.

"Thou art, indeed, forever lost to the world now, Coralie, but who can chide thee for choosing the better part, or dare pity thee, and look upon thy sweet face, lighted up with holiest joy, the reflection of the love and rapture filling thy heart in gratitude for being allowed to be the spouse of Christ."

A couple now advance and kneel beside her, to receive the blessing of the aged priest before them, and arise "man and wife."

Very beautiful did Viola look in the bashful timidity of her great happiness, as she was leaving the little church, leaning upon the arm of her husband. We will not follow them into their new life, but trust it will flow on smoothly and calmly, and that the love that fills the heart of the shrinking girl and the strong man supporting her, will continue to increase, and be the shield and comfort of their lives here, and attain a happy fruition in the life hereafter.

Preceding them are Col. and Mrs. Graham. A peaceful serenity shines in their features, and as now they too are happy, we will bid them adieu also. Near them are their children—the young doctor and his wife. A happiness not of earth is brightening their faces. Dr. George has that morning for the first time received the "Bread of Life," and he feels all the transports of that great joy, whilst Mary's heart is full of thanksgiving. Following them is a lonely-looking man, with an expression of pain and despair in his face. Need we say it is Alfred? We would fain linger longer near him, until peace and hope are stamped upon his brow—but our time is limited.

There are only two more of whom we need speak, and they are slowly leaving the chapel—the sister-in-law and the mother.

Poor Sallie! As she lifts her veil to offer feebly her congratulations to the newly-made man and wife we start at the sad changes wrought in that once lovely face by disease and suffering. But in spite of the great pock-marks, which are many, there is now a gentleness in those black eyes which captivates, and a softness of the whole exterior which makes us admire her infinitely more than we did the charmingly beautiful Sallie of yore.

What must we say of the mother who feels herself cruelly forsaken, and who is now weeping bitterly over what she imagines to be her child's desertion? Ah! Mrs. Caroline, those tears of distress will soon be dried. Even now, amidst your sorrow, thoughts of the comforts that would be yours were you to accept the offer of "hand and heart" made by that dashing Col. Clayton, are filling your mind, and before you reach your carriage you will have decided to make them yours. So we will say farewell to thee also.

THE END.

www.ingramcontent.com/pod-product-compliance
Lightning Source LLC
Chambersburg PA
CBHW021857230426
43671CB00006B/427